Trumping Imperialism

Nicholas O'Kelley

"If there is cultural imperialism, it is definitely American." – John Quelch

Prologue

Donald Trump is President. I do not believe I could formulate a more surprising and yet completely true statement if I sat here at the computer for another few days and yet, it remains surreal and nearly unbelievable. Do not take me wrong, I voted for the Donald, campaigned for him, and remain extremely happy with my choice to do so; this book is the furthest thing from some form of buyer's remorse or angry dossier where you read my rantings for the next few chapters centered around how the world is set to come to an end and we are all doomed. In fact, my goal is to outline exactly the opposite.

It should be addressed up front, however, that I am among the minority in writing something positive about the 45th President. In fact, if you would like to hear an onslaught of character assassination and unrelenting attacks on Trumps foreign or domestic policies, Tweets, pseudo imperialistic nature, and so on, I suggest you stop reading here and instead turn on the television to MSNBC or CNN. I am sure the likes of Rachel Maddow or Wolf Blitzer will better suit your intellectual requirements.

I am constantly perplexed by the refusal of the left to take one collective breath and realize that their rioting and general shenanigans will not change the fact that Hilary Clinton lost the election. It seems to me that the communal fear of Trump, pulsing through the liberal circulatory system of the country, has only accelerated since he took office and quite frankly, I cannot make sense of it. Is it simply driven by Hilary's recent viral videos reminding her constituents to keep standing up against hate? Is it that the last eight years under Obama have been so divisive that the country is unable to find its identity when starved of a white house touting racial discrimination?

What is going on that has created this population of oblivious, uneducated, liberal individuals who literally fall on their knees, screaming in the middle of the road on inauguration day, ransack a Starbucks, and beat admitted Trump voters bloody demanding that they receive equal rights as women? Maybe I have amnesia, but I do not remember ever owning or operating a DeLorean, I thought this was 2017. Did I just go back in time to 1919, before the Nineteenth Amendment was ratified? I was almost positive that women have equal rights, but maybe common core curriculums are older than I thought and my history education in school was grounded in complete inaccuracy.

My point is that Trump campaigned on America first. He was on the campaign trail in Wisconsin pushing the idea of buying American, he is working to bring back manufacturing jobs, trillions have been added to the stock market, and yet we remain in the first year of his administration. In what world are the naysayers living that these are not omens of confidence for the future?

Since I was a young man, studying in a small, private college, I have been arguing that the country has been turned into one giant corporation. Not to say that I am happy about it, but nevertheless, with a 20 trillion dollar budget, we have to admit to ourselves that the administrative tasks required at this point within Washington can no longer be entrusted to the bureaucracy of crony career politicians who have been bought off by special interests. Ask yourself how it is possible that John McCain, a literal troll living under a bridge named the golden gate rhino, built with neo-conservative concrete, manages to achieve re-election time after time? Are the people of Arizona so stupid that they don't realize how controlled he is by the military industrial complex? I do not think so, in fact, I suggest a simpler explanation.

John McCain makes so much money within the system and has so many internal donors and supporters that he exerts a power over the democratic system which does not allow for competition. He, like several tech companies of our time, which I will mention later on, has become the embodiment of a political trust, a monopoly if you will. It was my understanding that laws existed which protected our capitalistic nature in America against such an institution. Is it not the right time for a trust buster to once again take up residence in the White House? Someone who will put the interests of America first, rather than those of the United Nations?

Enter Donald Trump, the opposite of a crony politician and most likely the only businessman living today who could have accomplished a feat which remains nearly impossible; Wounding the Washington machine to such an effective extent that he literally exploded through the door of the American political system unscathed and begging for more. He said it himself, that we would bust through the ceiling of the main stream media, the mouthpiece of the left, and force Washington to once again work for the American people and drain the swamp. I remain confident that he is and will continue to do just that, break up the trusts built and maintained by the corrupt politicians and return order to the federal government. Will we agree with all of his methods? Certainly not, but the question we must ask ourselves before flying off the handle is, do we disagree because we do not understand his methods, or because they are wrong? At the end of the day, Donald Trump is an extremely successful businessman and he did not realize that title without a gainful ability to manage. To be honest, I have not seen a successful manager in the White House during my lifetime. I do not know what that is going to look like. I do however have a great idea of what it should look like and based on what I have seen so far, I think it is time to pen it down and watch it unfold.

In my opinion, there are two types of politicians, those who do not compromise (which are often those who do not remain in politics very long), and those who compromise too much. The Bush's, the Clinton's, Obama, to which category do you think they belong? They are all the same, republican, democrat, they all play for the same team; let me give you a hint, it is not the home team. Why else would NAFTA have been created? The giant sucking sound which now, years later, has proven Ross Perot to be a man of great intelligence far ahead of his time. Detroit wasting away like a third world country, unemployment rampant for Americans. Notice I said Americans? It does not look so bad for the illegal immigrants. After all, if they were unable to find gainful employment here, the problem would not continue to persist. NAFTA under Bill Clinton, the war for natural resources and imperialism under George W. and continued under Obama, which has subsequently created the refugee crisis that now threatens our very way of life. Can you honestly say that these are agendas implemented with American interests in mind? What could possibly drive a commander in chief to support such atrocities besides blackmail or the promise of money and power?

With this book, I intend to argue the case against the status quo which seems to frighten the liberal, democratic left so much. I will debunk the idea that a Donald Trump White House means a new imperialism in America and prove that his administration will secure the future of the country, rather than send it into a death spiral we would have no doubt seen under Hilary. The Constitution was not written and ratified by politicians, but rather by Statesmen, Engineers, Innovators, and Businessmen. The government was meant to be run by the people, for the people, not by the cronies, for the cronies.

I hear it all the time that Trump has no experience as a politician and we are in for World War III because he will stop at nothing to force himself upon the world. That Trump is a tyrant the likes of Hitler and Stalin and nationalism is a sin we must avoid at all cost. Why am I no longer allowed to take pride in my country? Why can I not be excited and proud about a dynasty of wealth built by the freedom we enjoy in America? Why can I not say America first? I do not want my tax money rebuilding the Middle East, supplying guns to Mexican drug cartels, and providing sex change operations to confused soldiers. I want my money rebuilding roads in America, creating jobs for Americans which will ultimately help balance the national budget, and offering health care to wounded warriors who fought for our freedom, sacrificed their lives to secure our borders, and harbor no uncertainty of who or what they are.

I do not have faith that any of these objectives would have been accomplished under Hilary Clinton, the demon succubus of Fleet Street, but I can and am glad to put my confidence in someone of Trump's stature. A blue collar billionaire indeed, but one who cares more about people than money. A man who works 18 hours a day, unlike Obama who may have had a phone and a pen, but who more often indulged a golf club. Therefore I ask a simple question to kick off the following chapters, what does the imperialism of America look like under Trump? Will our interests be protected at home, or will our influence be extended overseas? I intend to show that he will instead bring a balance to the force and through the next four to eight years, together, we will truly make America great again.

Chapter 1
The Trump Effect

Since Donald Trump was elected, a strange and exciting phenomenon has taken hold over the entire country; collective optimism. Ask yourself, when was the last time you as a citizen of America felt as though we were a great nation? Let me guess, it was probably sometime around the moment when George W. Bush declared War on Terrorism with those infamous words, "If you are not with us, then you are with the terrorists."

I will admit it, I was chanting "U.S.A" along with the rest of my conservative family and friends, but at the same time, I was still in high school, extremely naive, and somewhat stupid to be so blind to the obvious truth; what is your excuse? That is right, the truth I speak of is centered around the attack on the World Trade Center being perpetrated by Saudi Arabians, rather than Afghan radicals as we were led to believe. Why in the world would George W. allow such a ridiculous and expensive retaliation on a country innocent in the atrocities committed against our country?

In short, it was an agenda, carried out simply to radicalize individuals living in the Middle East in an attempt, now proven to be successful, to incite violence against the West and instill fear into the hearts of millions. A boogeyman, so to speak, was brought to life in that "Shock and Awe" firebombing that gave an excuse to thousands of Middle Eastern men to wage Jihad on the West.

At the end of the day, I would say that the Bush administration did a fantastic job. Most people believe the main stream narrative that Iraq and Afghanistan was a necessary move on our part, to serve justice for bringing down the towers and of those who don't, the majority believe it was all about oil. The truth, of course, lies somewhere in between.

We did indeed find a way to sit on top of the natural resources of the Middle East, once we had imposed our will in the area and destabilized the entire region, but of course, the boogeyman, in turn, gave an excuse to the American government to wage perpetual war against the Jihadists.

Only until such a time that they could be brought down of course, but to this day, it seems that task has not yet been accomplished.

I say all of that simply to set up an important question, were you proud of this nation when Bush authorized "Shock and Awe?" Did you feel that we were indeed a great country at that moment while watching Iraq burn to the ground as if it were Berlin in WWII? It was terrorism which brought our country together, united we stood watching the military industrial complex waste tax payer dollars while lying directly to our faces about it. Collective hatred had brought us a sense of pseudo patriotism that lasted for nearly a decade, so were we not a great country then?

If you were not proud during the Bush years, were you perhaps proud of our country under Obama? After all, he perpetuated the exact same agenda started by Bush, to fragment the Middle East and control it like a colony. After promising to bring the troops home, he sent in more. He, along with the help of Hilary Clinton, instigated the Arab Spring, which included such atrocities as the overthrow of the Egyptian and Libyan governments in order to install the Muslim Brotherhood, the subsequent attack on the Benghazi consulate and then lying to the American people about it, and implementing an agenda to depose Bashar Al Assad, one which is still being pushed by the war hungry Neo-Cons in Congress. Do these things not prove America's greatness?

I submit that racial division and war time profiteering are nothing to be proud of, regardless of the instant gratification it may bring with it. As Americans we pay a lot of taxes, it feels good to see that money going to securing our borders, a.k.a., expanding our interests abroad under the guise of freedom and sharing the wealth. However, that collective hate, as I described it before, can only last for so long. Lies built on lies, deceit, and political sabotage are morally unhealthy and at some point, the toxic sludge fills up the soul of a nation and starts to spill over into internal, domestic destruction.

Do you think I am wrong? Let us examine the last couple of years of the Obama administration. We saw the burning of Ferguson, Missouri while gangs of "protestors" marched through the streets, ransacked store fronts, and set fire to anything they felt like over the shooting of Michael Brown. The entire "Hands up don't shoot" slogan was born out of the lie that Brown was an innocent, walking away from a police officer calmly. When the truth came out that he was an armed thug who lunged for the officer's gun before being shot, it mattered not to the liberal left when they used this incident to incite violence throughout the country. Where was Obama when all of this was going on? Was he on the television calling for calm and reminding the American people that we are all one nation under God, indivisible? Or was he instead bolstering the violence, claiming the need for reform within the police departments across the country?

I am not here to make a case for the police. I support civil servants, I understand their plight in the line of fire and appreciate their service, nevertheless, no one is perfect and certainly, there are plenty of dirty, guilty cops within the system. The point is simply that a weak President, spouting supportive propaganda of criminal activity and then changing the subject to a red line in Syria is no way to drum up morale among the ranks. Like covering a bullet wound with a band aid, the infection will spread until all cancer has been removed; as is evident from the continued rioting and violence now known as the modus operandi of Black Lives Matter.

Do not be anxious, I am not driving to the statement that Donald Trump is the solution to all of our problems, but are you not tired of being told that our success as a nation does not belong to us and that the spoils of our hard work should go to revitalizing the infrastructure in the Middle East? After all, the only reason a restoration is needed is that the Bush, Clinton, and Obama regimes insisted on aligning themselves with Saudi Arabia and taking part in installing the Muslim Brotherhood to power in the Middle East. They put our country and our citizens at risk and for what? How could I possibly support Hilary Clinton after years of this instigation and pork belly spending to accomplish nothing more than meddling in foreign affairs? Not to mention that in parallel, they strong armed Congress into passing unfair trade agreements the likes of NAFTA, which not only destroyed Detroit but also shipped the majority of manufacturing overseas and left us with an unemployment rate hovering somewhere around 40%.

You read right, not 4.0%, as the Democrats would have you believe, 40%. Hilary Clinton and Obama called that figure ridiculous when Trump brought it up during the Presidential debates in 2016, in fact, Hilary kept reminding viewers like you to keep the fact checking going as if that would somehow discredit him completely. Contrary to popular belief and lucky for us, the public was able to see past that shadow campaign and it is not hard to understand why. The American people are fed up with career politicians and the status quo. They know something is wrong when Hilary claims she and Bill came out of the White House completely broke and yet she owns multiple mansions worth seven figures. Can you truly say that you relate to Hilary Clinton? Where do you think she gets that money from, hard work?

Being a career politician is an extremely lucrative business venture. When you make the laws, it is easy to manipulate the flow of tax dollars into your own pocket. Take Joe Biden for example. His son Hunter, a lawyer, lobbyist, and private citizen joined the board of the largest natural gas company in the Ukraine, Burisma Holdings, back in April of 2014. It was not but around a year later when the then Vice President was in the Ukraine preaching about corruption and explaining to the leaders of the country the benefits of limiting the power of the oligarchs. Evidently, he is not one to walk the talk. Imagine it, you are the Vice President and somehow your lawyer son is able to sit on a foreign board of directors for an oil company? I wonder what experience and skills they felt Hunter Biden harbored which would benefit their business? You think his political ties had anything to do with it? Or is it his obvious knowledge of business and drilling technology that gave him such a controversial position?

Trump's promise was to drain the swamp. The grimy, corruption filled cesspool, bubbling in Washington that has fed foreign interests for far too long and it will absolutely take someone outside of the system to pull the plug. The American people are tired of under-handed deals driving government policies, such as the appointment of Biden, and we, therefore, put our faith in someone so far outside of the system, the left thought they could bring him down with a simple smear campaign. I am proud to say that it did not work and after pondering on it for some time, I have finally understood why. It is not his success as a real estate mogul or his lavish lifestyle, it is not his super model wife or private plane that gives the American people confidence in Trump. Those traits would work for cheap car salesmen or a cookware peddler, but with Donald Trump, it is something much simpler, something much more real.

Trump is a real person, a billionaire, yes, but a real, red-blooded American. He prefers a Nathan hot dog over a dish of caviar, likes steak and potatoes, and cares about the people who work for him, not because of the publicity, but because he wants people to be happy and successful. What did you think The Apprentice was all about? Why do you think he has adorned the Oval Office with gold curtains to match the molding in the New York penthouse he has grown so accustomed to? Donald Trump believes in the American dream, he believes that if people are provided the proper motivation and support, they can truly develop from rags to riches.

Ladies and gentlemen, I am here to tell you the honest truth as best as I can describe it. We, as a country, have fallen utterly and completely into rags and unfortunately, Chapter 11 is not an option. The globalist agenda that has taken deep root in Washington and thus the entire country wants to keep you poor. The goal is to suck the country dry of money and resources, funneling that cash into the pockets of big businesses, special interests, and foreign, U.N. agendas while the American people pay for it. It is maddening for the American people to work themselves to death and then be told every evening by Fox News that the economy is crashing and the country is broke. Not to mention that in the same breath, the media reports record tax collection year after year by Congress. What is wrong with this picture? It is very simple and I have already provided the answer.

America, your politicians, the ones who are supposed to represent us in Congress, have instead been representing whoever pays the most money. While given the statistics it is easy to assume that American tax payers are the highest donor, the reality is very different. The truth is that your taxes pay the interest on our 20 trillion dollar debt.

Now, if you have student loans as I do, you know that the interest payment does nothing but keep your credit score static and that remaining balance statement looms month after month, reminding you that you simply do not make enough money to really get ahead at the ATM. In the same way, you can imagine why it is that those record tax collection reports are completely irrelevant to a senator. If your taxes were paying their salaries, you can believe that the term "career politician" would not exist.

Their wealth is instead generated by lobbyists, big business, and special interest groups with deep pockets who have vested interests in seeing legislation that directly benefits their profit margin. Have you ever asked yourself why it is that Google is allowed to hide money overseas to avoid domestic taxes? Have you ever wondered why we have companies in Silicon Valley admittedly worth more than the GDP of entire countries and yet somehow the U.S. is in debt 20 trillion dollars? Tax evasion is a simple operation when it is made legal by Congressional legislation and it is easy to buy votes in Congress when politicians can be bought off. As the old additive states, "Money talks."

The President of the United States is in reality no different than the Congress men and women. I remember being blown away by the amount of money reported that it took for Obama to buy the Oval Office. The first billion dollar presidential race in history and he simply outspent the competition in my opinion. Look it up, Obama raised 750 million dollars to run for President in 2008 and in 2012, proceeds broke 1 billion. The key word there, of course, is "raised," not spent out of his own bank account or sold cakes and pies at a bake sale to make his campaign possible, "raised." You can believe that means money was donated from Wall Street with the sole intent of purchasing a Presidential agenda. There is no other explanation for the systematic shutdown of the southern border by Obama and the executive action that subsequently allowed for the mass migration of illegal immigrants into the country.

Do you honestly believe Obama cared so much about the people of Mexico that he would accept them as refugees? How can that be true anyway, when it was the Fast and Furious scandal, led by Obama and Eric Holder, which armed the drug cartels with American weapons and created the refugee crisis south of the border in the first place? When you first heard about Fast and Furious, did you not find it strikingly similar to the destabilization campaign in the Middle East? Did you wonder why the Obama administration was not brought to justice for such an abomination? Are you asking yourself whether or not I am referring to a Vin Diesel movie?

Not that I want to take too much of a detour from the main point, but I think it is important to explain the illegal immigration situation. I think we can all agree it is a crisis. If you do not understand that allowing non-tax paying people into the country in such ridiculous amounts is not only a danger to our security but a huge risk to our economic stability, then I would like you to stop reading immediately and contact me directly. I would like to speak to you about buying some oceanfront property in Arizona that I have been sitting on for years. It is a great deal and I think the time is perfect to sell. For the rest of you, let us quickly examine the two main reasons that Obama committed this crime.

First of all, he wanted to create a voting bloc in the country to secure a win for the Democrats in future elections. If a Republican were to win in 2016, the jig would be up, Obama's corruption would unravel, and indictments would be served once the FBI was back under the control of the American people. Hint, hint, Jim Comey was fired by Trump, hint, hint, Barry's days are numbered. Why else would the Democrats push to allow voting without an ID, saying it was an infringement on our rights to ask for one? Do you agree with that? Is it not more of an infringement to not ask for an ID? If voting booths require an ID, then illegal immigrants cannot vote! The corruption in the government is so in your face it is crazy, but evidently they think we are just that stupid.

The second reason was to create a workforce of cheap labor. It is expensive to employ American's and I wonder if you have ever stopped to consider why? For one we work hard, American's only have two weeks of vacation per year and we, therefore, need to be compensated appropriately for the lack of work/life balance we harbor, at least in comparison to other countries. We are also a free society and that is not just a pseudo patriotic saying that makes me feel good, it actually means something.

You see, in America, there is no socialist government taking half of our money and then subsidizing our lives with handouts. We do pay a lot of taxes, 25-35% is unbelievable on our income, not to mention that the income tax is completely unconstitutional, but that is a point for another time. Nevertheless, some countries pay upwards of 50-60 percent! When the government imposes that amount of taxes on its citizens, it has to provide some aspects of daily life to compensate, for example, cheap cable, power, water, etc. American citizens pay for these things, giving us more choices and control of our own lives, but also requires that we make more money at work, in order to enjoy a higher quality of life.

The illegal immigrant population, in general, is not used to a higher pay or a high quality of life and are therefore more than willing to work for three dollars an hour, free housing, and tax exempt status. With McDonald's employees protesting now for 15 dollars an hour, it only makes sense that Facebook looks to employ illegals rather than "entitled" Americans; does that make sense to you? The sad part is that the protests at McDonald's are a direct result of NAFTA. As I mentioned before, that legislation shipped our jobs overseas. Did you know that manufacturing jobs are among the highest paying hourly jobs in the country, even today? The Washington Post recently reported that benefits, like health insurance and retirement, are higher per hour for factory workers and that wages were 17% higher on average due to more hours offered per week and more weeks of work offered per year.

The point is that if only the government was more interested in keeping Americans employed by creating real jobs, then large employers would not feel the need to hire cheap labor from the fear of a cyclical demand for higher wages. In the same way, if the government would discontinue the allowance of corporations to hire illegal immigrants, there would be more jobs for Americans and less would be forced into the retail/fast food industry, thus demanding jobs not intended for full-time employment to pay higher wages.

These examples paint a dark picture of the political landscape in the United States. One that, in my opinion, easily explains the unrest of the American people. We, as a whole, no longer feel appropriately represented by the government we pay for and as history shows, once there exists a taxation without representation on Americans, it is time to incite the Boston Tea Party. A show of strength and solidarity for American values, a call to arms which cries, "We have been overrun by foreign interests and we need to take back our republic and hang the traitors in the streets." That cry was echoed during the 2016 election and the result is Donald John Trump.

Ladies and Gentlemen, take pride, the Trump effect is in full swing and I promise that we the people can be excited for what is to come. I recently read a Paul Joseph Watson article at Infowars, which served as a fantastic list of Trump's accomplishments thus far. Shall I recap them here for you? Perhaps it will help explain to you why the blue collar workers of the United States once again feel represented, as though their interests are being adhered to, as though we will again make America great. The list goes as follows:

1. Job creation by U.S. employers, 238,000 in January and 235,000 in February, with the unemployment rate falling to 4.7% as mentioned before.
2. Cutting the federal debt by 68 billion dollars.
3. Trillions have been added to the stock market with record highs reported and the DOW surging 2500 points or 12% since the inauguration.
4. Manufacturing returning to the U.S. with companies including Exxon investing 20 billion in order to create 45,000 jobs, Fiat reporting an investment of 1 billion to create 2,000 jobs, Hasbro moving Play-Doh manufacturing back to the U.S., Samsung investing in 500 jobs, and the Carrier plant announcement to discontinue its move to Mexico.
5. The rollback of Obama era regulations which were shutting down industries including the end of regulations on coal and the executive order to kill the Trans Pacific Partnership.
6. Trump has issued an executive order to end sanctuary cities and illegal immigration as a whole is down 40 percent.
7. The repeal and replacement of Obamacare have been started and international funding for abortions has been discontinued by the federal government.
8. Trump has approved the Dakota Access and Keystone Pipelines which will create more jobs and reduce gas costs.
9. Trump has nominated Neil Gorsuch to the Supreme Court, a strong constitutionalist, to replace the late Antonin Scalia, which effectively hands the voting majority of the Supreme Court back to the American people.

This is of course only a short list of accomplishments, but I dare you to find something here which is outside of the interests of the American people. Could you compile such an impressive list after Obama's first 100 days? Could you compile such a list after his first 8 years? Donald Trump is not and seemingly cannot be bought off. He paid for his presidential campaign with his own money, meaning that his agenda is his own, the agenda he promised to the people, to turn the government back over to them. As you can see, at least I hope that you can, he is doing just that. Not compromising, taking the money, and running, but working hard to implement an agenda of restoring the republic and making America great again. Did you feel that swell of pride when you read that last sentence? It is not a draft from the open window...it is the Trump effect.

Chapter 2
Trump and the Propaganda Machine

Where would we be had Hilary Clinton been elected? Think about that for a moment, then come back here and let me know what you come up with. Did you say to yourself, "at war with Russia?" I did. Let us put aside for a moment the issue of North Korea and the actual possibility of war very soon. I am not oblivious, I understand that tensions are high and certainly the dear leader is attempting to either legitimately start WWIII or, just really wants to win a pissing contest with Trump.

For the record, neither of those scenarios is a good idea for him. They fire off a missile every few weeks, in direct defiance of the wishes of China and the warnings coming from the U.S., but this is nothing new. It is merely the perpetuation of a tradition started by his grandfather to prove the military dominance of North Korea. We all know it is insane and any actual war between North Korea and the United States would be swift and decisive, at least in the case that Trump is the commander in chief. The question for me, however, is not how quickly can we bring down the communist state, but rather is it required?

The liberals would love to see Trump start a war in Korea, I can smell the spin now; talking point would, without doubt, abide entailing such statements as, "We told you so," "Trump is a war-monger," "Trump is a fascist," and "Trump will not stop until he conquers the world." Comparisons to Hitler have already been relentless from the media, an actual conflict would no doubt fuel the fire, regardless of the actual necessity. Granted, I do not want to see another conflict in Korea, but I much prefer a strong stance from the Donald, rather than the blind eye approach enlisted by Obama for so many years.

Nevertheless, can we not all admit that, at the very least, Trump is not pursuing a course of action which would lead us to an unnecessary war? The conflict with North Korea has been instigated and fueled by none other than the North Koreans. If he takes action, which in my opinion is not the President's preference, it would be justified, necessary, and a long time coming, so to speak.

The difference between this potential conflict and a full on the war waged against Russia, which would have no doubt been started by a Clinton administration, is that war with Russia is neither necessary nor in the best interest of our country or any of our allies! I ask you, am I wrong? Do you disagree? If not, then can someone please tell me why the Democrats and proponents of the military industrial complex are foaming at the mouth for military action against Putin? On second thought, do not answer that, it is a rhetorical question. I am writing this book after all, so sit down and I will tell you why.

The fact is, we all know the reason the politicians want war with Russia. It creates more back door contracts for war time manufacturers, it gives the career politicians such as Lindsey Graham and John McCain a platform for re-election, and it would further destabilize a country attempting to rebuild itself before they become a legitimate competition on the global market. Not to mention that Russia holds vast stores of natural resources.

Imagine after centuries free of defeat the United States is solely responsible for the demise of General Winter. I can practically smell the drool leaking from the side of Hilary Clinton's stroked out mouth and if I am being honest, it smells like desire. How else do you explain the blitzkrieg from the media against Russia? The desperate attempt to link Trump and Putin with no concrete ground to even stand on? I feel like we have been transported back to the early 1980's and it is unbelievably insane!

This is, to my point, however, the charge of the mainstream media. They have been tasked to use talking points and repetition to alter reality in such a way that the American people are no longer able to form logical conclusions for themselves about current events. Remember back in school when the teacher would ask you to clip articles from the newspaper and present current events to the class in order to discuss them or, god forbid, even debate them? I am curious to know how many teachers today still employ that practice. I wonder how many students are actually given the opportunity to study current events, rather than the bastardized historical ones found in liberal text books. I would wager that the answer is none, in fact, I would bet the house on it. And, for the few teachers who do enlist such heinous aggressions, I can only imagine a number of complaints from left-wing parents and calls for dismissal which would likely follow from the school board.

Ladies and gentlemen, the unfortunate circumstance we now face, especially after eight years of Obama, is that education based in reality is no longer the goal of any institution of learning within liberal America. Please do not take me wrong, it has nothing to do with not wanting to teach kids, in fact, the truth is just the opposite. The desire to teach the younger generation radiates from the left like a warm crater of kryptonite. The problem is that they do not wish to offer a factual curriculum centered on historical evidence, but instead strive to provide one of propaganda designed to prepare a young mind to willingly accept a "bag of goods," if you will. Needless to say, Joseph Goebbels would be proud of the standards found currently in states such as California. Let me expand on this a little further.

The "liberal" message is one of chaos and self-destructive behavior. It seeks only to centralize control within the government, sell off the arsenal of assets throughout the country to the highest bidder, and then generate a massive, undeserved payday for those at the top. Sound familiar? Turn on the history channel and watch a show about the old monarchies of Europe, you know, the kind our fore father's escaped from in order to build this land we now take for granted.

How can the left possibly expect anyone to buy such a proverbial "bag of goods" when it is so obviously detrimental to our constitutionally protected rights and way of life? After all, any reasonable person with an ability to institute common sense into a normal thought process would understand the difference between an agenda of freedom and prosperity and one that wishes to bring America to its knees, offering our democracy up to a new world order, right?

Oh wait, was that too much for you? Are you saying to yourself, "he is crazy?" Allow me to present a couple of examples to illustrate this illustrious bag you are holding and what exactly the type of goods is that it contains. First of all, let us begin with the fact that China is buying a stake in Hollywood to gain influence over the American people. That is right, this is not speculation, just google "China buying up Hollywood" and let me know what you get returned. Did you find the article about the richest man in China buying part ownership into Sony Pictures? How about the Wanda Group in China buying the studio, Legendary Entertainment, or even a BBC article asking about whether or not the Chinese interest in Hollywood has anything to do with gaining soft influence in America?

I am simply unable to understand how the American government can abide such a travesty and this is only one example. Recently there have been many instances of foreign billionaires and governments buying up land in the American Midwest, "rescuing" failing businesses, and buying an interest in every type of company from hotels down to breweries. All of them systematically being gobbled up by Chinese, Japanese, Saudi Arabian, and European interests as if the world was a game of Hungry, Hungry, Hippos and we were the beads. Why? I would think that the answer is obvious, but perhaps I need to state it anyway: The American people are poor!

Do you remember in the last chapter that I mentioned the destruction of American manufacturing thanks to NAFTA? The fact that the employment gap was forcing the middle class into retail, fast food, or even worse, early retirement? Well, believe it or not, this has a massive effect on the overall economy. Think about it. If the middle class does not have as much money, then there is less demand for new shoes, new clothes, new appliances, new cars, and even new electronics. With less money comes more of a need for larger loans and higher credit limits, which causes more debt, which leads ultimately to more foreclosures and default, you know how it goes.

Does any of this ring a bell? Does anyone remember 2008? I ask you, how were we able to fix that problem? Raise your hand if you know, or did you just assume the cash fairy landed on the government's proverbial pillow one night and shed her green skin as a sacrifice on the altar of freedom. If that was the case, then let me offer you a shot of reality, you may want to remain seated for this one.

From what I remember, the Federal Reserve printed more money and your tax dollars propped up the central banks. Meanwhile, Obama convinced you that raising the debt limit was simply good business, just something that had to be done every once in a while in order to make sure that the government stayed open and kept doing their job to protect the American people. If only we had all realized the irony of that statement at the time, we would have revolted and allowed the government to get shut down. After all, the states can govern themselves.

We do not need the federal government, it exists only to deprive you of certain inalienable rights, granted in the Constitution I might add, under the guise of keeping you safe. Seriously, imagine the irony that we surrendered more tax dollars to keep the government open for security and yet by the end of the Obama presidency, the country was in the worst possible position of its short history. The economy was in the toilet, the terror threats were at a critical point, and the population was on the verge of a civil war, where it, unfortunately, remains as Trump calls for peace and tries to reign in the division. This, however, is a topic for another time.

My overall point here is that you and I are in even more debt than ever before and the government, rather than balancing the budget and cutting out the fat, is looking for more ways to sell us out and rake in more mullah. Admitting defeat would only halt the gravy train and given the lack of actual skills found amongst most of the career politicians, you can believe that would ensure their certain demise. "Full steam ahead" they cry, while our wallets suffer and they get a good laugh on the way to the bank. This was of course until very recently, when Trump came to town.

Does this explain to you why the swamp so desperately needs a good draining? Does it explain why the swamp is fighting so viciously back against Trump? Any government willing to sell its citizen's hard earned prosperity for a quick buck deserves the gallows and if it were up to me, I would pull the lever myself.

Regardless, China buying us out is merely a small issue, if you can even believe that. I am more interested in a different sale which was perpetrated a short time ago and it will serve as my second example. Perhaps you will remember when Hilary Clinton was caught selling off one-fifth of the U.S. uranium deposits in exchange for donations to the Clinton Foundation? I believe the figure was something to the tune of 145 million dollars. Can you believe that is even a real news story? Imagine my anger when, having knowledge of foreign governments buying our assets, I find out that at the same time, our politicians are intentionally selling off natural resources. Then imagine how it could be possible that my anger is not mirrored within the American political system! How can so many people blindly protest a platform of America first when the alternative is further destruction of our once proud nation?

How can they be against someone like Trump who is attempting to give the power back to the people and instead ask for Hilary? It is like the people asking for Barabbas to be released and Jesus to be hung on a cross. I often think to myself that it must be a mistake, nevertheless, it is the truth, it is factual, but in my mind, it is most certainly not "satisfactual."

Let us think about it for just a second, ponder with me if you will. Hilary Clinton is in part if not completely, responsible for the false accusations surrounding Donald Trump and collusion between his administration and the Russian government. How is it that Congress continues to waste tax payer time and money on this ludicrous investigation, but yet nothing has been mentioned about indicting Hilary over her obvious pay for play schemes? How she is not the one under investigation for collusion with Russia when she gave them our uranium I can simply not fathom. Not to mention, how is it possible that the Obama administration allowed something so stupid? In what world does it make sense that the Clintons war monger about a conflict with Russia and in the same breath sell them uranium? Am I crazy? No, I am not crazy, in fact, the very ability to question these issues proves my mental clarity. I write this book to offer the same lucidity to you because the reality is, a massive propaganda machine has been built in America, constructed by the very entities I speak of in our government for one purpose. To detract from the obviousness of this reality and to hide the corruption from the American people, but we will speak more about it in a few minutes, so stick around.

Getting back to the point, at this juncture, it is practically beyond reproach that the Clinton Foundation existed solely as a favor for hire banking system, which admittedly took money from foreign governments and in exchange provided information, back door deals, and evidently, even resources! This is treason! This is insane! And what is even more mesmerizing is the fact that she remains a free citizen. This is also why you now see such a push for Chelsea Clinton in the media.

Have you not wondered where she came from after all these years? Of course, she has always been lurking in the shadows like some creeping sex offender, but it was not until recently when, in my opinion, Hilary began to smell stiff competition that Chelsea started hitting the MSM news circuit a little more heavily. I nearly puked to see the forced perspective still shot photo of the Clinton's exiting the hospital. You all saw it, right? The picture rousing comparisons between her child bearing and that of the royal family. The one that looked nearly identical to the famous photo from London? Go look it up if you are unfamiliar, you will see what I mean. Did you gag like I did, or am I just a little too sensitive to propaganda?

I digress, all of a sudden, Chelsea is winning awards, being presented on the front page of magazines, and giving speeches for hundreds of thousands of dollars, just as Hilary is losing her political clout. Coincidence? I think not, this is no accident, let me assure you. This is by design and fully intended as an attempt to retain proximity to the government in order that the Clinton Foundation maintain its profit share worldwide. If favors are not possible, then profit will not be made available, at least according to the business model they have disseminated thus far. The joke is, however, on them in my opinion as Chelsea Clinton certainly does not have enough charisma or charm to carry the load and certainly not enough to get into office.

Nevertheless, I have begun to understand the literal meaning behind the phrase, "go big or go home," while watching politics throughout the past couple of decades, most specifically, while watching the Clintons. I mean, if I was to steal a few candy bars from the local drugstore, I would be locked up in a maximum security prison. At the same time, the Clintons continue to steal votes, trade favors for wealth, use a private server to improperly handle classified documents, sell out our country and the American people, on a massive scale I might add, and then walk free. All the while they laugh in our face and incite more violence and protests against the current commander in chief who, by contrast, has nothing but good intentions for his constituents. It took Trump months to even fire Jim Comey, the guy that opened an investigation into Hilary in order that he save face, only to close it a week later saying that he found no evidence of any wrongdoing. Seriously? The FBI found no issue with Hilary

Clinton, but yet Comey himself perpetuated this Russian investigation in the media with his promise of "notes" and the Trump dossier for months? I ask you now, what do we have to show for all of the frustration and mud-slinging? Nothing.

So then, back to my question, why did it take so long for Trump to get rid of Comey? Why does there remain so many Obama holdovers who are clearly the reason for the never-ending leaks and headaches in the Trump administration? The answer is simple. Trump gives people the benefit of the doubt. He believes in the power of the people and the human spirit. Trump wants to empower the American public to get back to work and live better lives. A stark contrast to the former administration I know, but the intentions are clear.

Trump wants you to be smart and make decisions for yourself, Obama thinks you're stupid. Obama wants the state to give you the news, Trump wants to tear down the fake news behemoth and let you analyze the facts for yourself. Trump is a real president, Obama is a puppet. Can you sense a pattern here? Let me make it easier, Trump is a conservative libertarian, Obama is a left-wing liberal.

If I have not made it clear enough, I will try to boil it down a little further. The liberal agenda aims to pull the wool over your eyes to mask rampant corruption and keep you focused on trivial issues, such as the Russian collusion and interference with the election of Trump. We voted for Donald Trump my friends, not Russia. Do not let these charlatans fool you. They only want to keep the public locked in a virtual matrix, happy and stupid and for those who escape, to play off of their emotions with divisive agendas so that we all fight amongst ourselves. Meanwhile, they mask the real end game as "progressivism," which ensures the hordes of trendy millennials and their elder, flower child, drug addict parents and grandparents jump on board with no questions asked.

That real objective of course merely centers on greed. Your elected, career politicians have been given immense power over the general population. Think about it. How long has John McCain and Nancy Pelosi been in office? How much good has Lindsey Graham actually done for the state of South Carolina? When was the last time a failure to pass a law, take the health care bill for example, kept the Congress from taking 30 days of vacation off, multiple times a year? How many of you have 30 days with which to take a vacation each year, much less more than once?

These rhino republicans and liberal democrats do not fight for your rights or the well-being of the country, they fight to keep themselves in office. Otherwise, they will lose that massive payday and those tax afforded benefits you and I pay so lovingly for. Thusly, we have reached a Sodom and Gomora style turning point with our government. Let me take a moment to broaden your mind because it is of the up most importance that you leave this chapter with a full understanding of what I am saying.

The members of government in America have been bought off. It is not so difficult to imagine when you think about it. They write the legislation which governs our democracy and therefore, they become a natural target for those with money who wish to control the ways and means by which we are governed. In the past, these entities have been limited to lobbies, maintained for the most part by restrictive laws, which ensured that their influence was known, but not all powerful. This is a historic concept which, though still in existence, has been outweighed now by the 1% or the very small circle of individuals who control the majority of the wealth in the world and wish to use that fact to gain leverage over the general population. Is it necessary that I name these people? I think their companies are a household name, most of which are contributing to the alternative reality you and I now live in; You know, the one in which the propaganda of the left is leading you to believe that everything is awesome? That everything is cool when you are part of the team, to quote the great film, The Lego Movie.

The issue is that these "1%'ers," which I only use as a colloquial reference for the readers to understand to whom I am referring (the reality is a much smaller percentage) have now taken near full control of the talking points and agendas on the floor of Congress. Until now, this was also true on the floor of the white house, but as Trump said himself on numerous occasions, he paid for his own campaign and is therefore not accountable to special interests. Oh, I apologize, were you not aware of what special interests meant? I forget that political jargon is often lost on the public, considering that is why it is used in the first place, to be confusing.

Special interests make up any group, which is not a formal lobby, but yet manage to influence politicians through large donations and favors granted at an opportune time, in order that they win candidacies and are then seated in a position of power. You scratch my back and I will scratch yours sort of agreement which has ensured that the real puppet masters of our democracy, the "1%," chose our leaders for us, while at the same time funding a propaganda machine with which to both hide themselves and offer us, the "99%," the illusion of choice and free will. How else could community organizers with no real experience the likes of Barack Obama and Bernie Sanders, rise to power and run for the highest office in America? Why else would Donald Trump be the only candidate with enough money and fame to win the Presidency back from these globalist scum in a population of 326 million people? Is there no one else who cares enough about America to fill the void!? Is there truly no one else qualified beyond people like Mitt Romney and George W. Bush? Wait a moment, I just threw up in my mouth a little.

The answer to these questions lies within the current and tremendous suppression of We the People. Boys and girls, you have been had, you have been taken for a ride, swindled by highway robbers of the absolute worst kind. You now find yourself on a vacation to the Caribbean and pirates just stole your wallet, found your home, and robbed your safe. Let me be more specific. Career politicians and their handlers have instituted a propaganda machine in America, and incidentally an extremely successful one, built from the ground up that rivals the breadth of the Nazi regime tactics, but one that is better disguised within the confines of social networking, television, news, college courses, all the way down to grade school.

Indeed, in case you were not yet aware, the left wing in America today, led by the Democratic Party and known socialist/communist financiers like George Soros, have systematically taken over education and information dissemination with only one goal in mind: to program people from an early age to their dying breath, with any and all propaganda that denounces freedom. Fake news which seeks to remove your notion of governance by the people by inciting racial and cultural division to keep you busy and provide you with tabloid quality distractions that shift your focus to anything except current affairs. Why would you be interested in the corrupt, over-inflated budget Congress is passing with money given to illegal immigrants in the form of welfare and money given to expanding the NSA's data collection on you and your family, whenever there is so many women's marches, gay pride parades, and black lives matter riots to attend? Why would you want to get involved and contact your Congressmen about the decaying roads and bridges when you can watch Johnny Depp destroy himself or Gwyneth Paltrow ogle over Obama?

Now, many of the liberals reading this will no doubt, at the moment, be thinking to themselves how crazy I am, how stupid that statement sounds, and how racist and bigoted I must be to be writing such falsehoods. Do not worry, I already have some lawyers lined up to defend the inevitable discrimination case this will bring about. I can only imagine the class action against me from the entirety of the Democratic Party, but the reason for the backlash should be obvious. I am speaking the truth and that directly conflicts with the propaganda currently brainwashing liberal America from dawn until dusk. Truth and reality have been suppressed and replaced with virtual reality in the form of social media and, as Trump calls it, fake news. Thusly, statements such as "make America great again" have become bigoted, flying the Confederate flag and allowing Confederate statues to remain in place is considered racist, and free speech is only allowed to those who agree with socialist policies and are "open-minded" enough to accept the destruction of the family unit.

I ask you, is it not this mindset that you find while watching CNN that conservative views are old hat, irrational, and small-minded? Does common sense not give you a feeling of unease when you watch Stephen Colbert relentlessly bash Trump about wanting to build a wall? Have you ever thought to yourself, "Self, I think putting Americans back to work, deporting non-tax paying "dreamers," and rejecting the climate change bullies might make sense," only to be immediately confronted by Bill Maher who says that "the best thing you can do for the environment is to not produce another resource-sucking human?" This is the propaganda machine. This is the dehumanizing force that endeavors to tear down your will and build you back up slowly into a pathetic, socialist Oliver Twist begging "please government, may I have some more?"

This, my friends, is the reason we elected Donald John Trump. Not just to drain the swamp, but to break through the glass ceiling of disinformation and indoctrination built by the mainstream media and their owners to silence the middle class in America, obliterate our prosperity, and usher in a new age of indentured servitude. The world where the ruling class reaps all of the benefits and we the silent majority do nothing but eat, sleep, and produce. Is that the future you envision for your children? Because the cure to the disease is bottled and ready for shipment, in fact, it is residing in the White House this very minute.

Believe it or not, we voted him in, but the battle he faces is real, it will be long, and it cannot be won alone. We must reject this legion of falsehood and show our support for the President boldly. It is time to step out from behind the wall of trepidation, because the fact is, the only reason the phony media is still operating in America is that the masses continue to buy into their nonsense. If we truly wish to make America great again, we must stand up America, take up arms alongside Trump, and wage an information war against the oppressive propaganda machine.

Chapter Three
The Business of Politics

In my lifetime, there have been multiple instances in which I can recount a genuine learning experience from which an actual life lesson was manifested, one that I have truly kept. Notice that I did not say "many instances," but rather "multiple," and that is as honest of a statement as I can make on the subject. It has always annoyed me to hear people saying, "You learn something every day," because while you may indeed learn something new, how much of the new information acquired daily is legitimately useful? My head is so full of useless knowledge I could make money off of an almanac detailing the uselessness of the 21st century, how about you? Nevertheless, there is one experience in particular that I wish to share with the reading audience, a day in my life where my eyes were truly opened to the inner workings of the real world.

I was in high school. Do not ask me what year, I do not want to reveal my age and given the content of the story, the date is completely irrelevant anyway. I had recently been awarded my driver's license and on the day of my 16th birthday, my parents had lovingly supplied me with my first car, an olive green Dodge Stratus my Dad had driven for a few years. A fantastic car, a four door sedan with a four cylinder engine, it was great on gas and tough as nails. I later sold it at 210,000 miles and, as far as I know, it is running to this day.

I should note at this juncture that I have always had a substandard ability to engage in misconduct, a fact which made it particularly difficult to get away with anything as a child and young man, not that I often committed acts which necessitated expulsion, but nevertheless. I commonly found myself being subjected to the normal parental "talking to," as I am sure most of you are familiar with. My first days driving were no exception to this rule, in fact, I believe it was within the first week of venturing out on my own via auto in which this particular situation occurred.

I was running errands, one of which involved driving to the store and after making my purchases and returning to my car, I realized my next stop was just across the street. I was due at the groomer to retrieve my dog and unfortunately, I was running late for the appointment. I put the car in drive, pulled into the street, and prepared to enter immediately into the median in order to turn directly into the parking lot of my next stop. Before making the turn, however, I was greeted in my rear view mirror by the ever ominous blue lights of a city police vehicle.

You can imagine my horror as my brain raced through all possible explanations of why this cop was pulling me over. Had I sped into the median without realizing it? I had not even driven far enough to accumulate any real momentum. Perhaps I had pulled out in front of someone? There was certainly no stop light or sign which I had accidentally run, I had not gone into an intersection, much less crossed one. It was then that my eyes brought me to a clear understanding when I looked down at myself...I had forgotten to buckle my seat belt.

Such a simple task and yet, the persistent and unremitting slogan which had found its way onto billboards and into hours' worth of commercials, not to mention my dreams in the weeks leading up to the infamous DMV test, had somehow failed me in my most desperate hour, "Click it or ticket." The gods be damned! How could I have let this happen!? How could I have overlooked the most basic of car safety measures? It did not matter, however, as the policeman approached my car from the right-hand side, I prepared to accept my inevitable doom; a simple slip of paper that would definitely seal my fate for the rest of my life. A flick of the wrist for this officer, but a trip down a far reaching path to certain grounding and reproach from my parents which I, at this moment, had no idea how to explain to them.

The point of this story, however, has nothing to do with the life lesson of buckling your seat belt, though I highly encourage you to do so. Not only to avoid the relatively expensive ticket, but also for safety; come on people, cars are death traps, buckle up. The point is instead focused on what happened to me in the weeks following this ticket when I managed to "settle" the issue, shall we say.

Fast forward about two weeks in which time I managed to get in touch with a family friend who was a judge and friend of the city's legal system. They assured me that it was no problem and that they could help me nullify the ticket, fee, and the scarlet letter which was now squashing my permanent record, at least in my mind.

So, to make a long story short, they set me up with a lawyer who accompanied me to traffic court, where, for the first time in my life, I became aware of the real world. The glasses were removed from my eyes, an awakening occurred in my mind, the veil was lifted, and upon crossing the threshold into that rather dark, wood-floored bastion of justice, I realized that I had just run out of bubble gum (Some of you will get that reference). Ladies and gentlemen, what I found in that room was life altering.

Have you ever been to court? Have you ever seen the justice system really work? Not that you would want to, but if the opportunity ever presents itself to you, pay close attention, because what I am about to describe has immense relevance to the political atmosphere Donald Trump now finds himself immersed in.

It was a farce, a casino, a mob of swindlers, overseen by the Don, but yet authorized to wheel and deal and running amuck like I had never before been witness to. The thing is, when you watch cop dramas and legal based shows like Law and Order, you paint this picture for yourself of what the justice system looks like. I had, even though I have never really enjoyed that genre of television and yet when I entered into traffic court that day, I was blown away by the level of inaccuracy with which I had been bamboozled. First of all the defendants were, for the most part, not even in attendance. The court room looked normal, with a bar, an audience, two tables, and a judge, but the atmosphere was thick with deception.

I will never forget the judge, sitting behind the podium with his feet up on the desk, chatting it up with the attorney in front of him about the car he had evidently just restored. I thought to myself, "What is going on here?" but I was quickly hit with a dose of reality when the lawyer then changed the subject by saying, "so about this speeding ticket." The judge said, "100 bucks and tell them I do not want to see them in here again," though the perpetrator, as I mentioned, was not even in the room. Unbelievable to me, but nevertheless, I received nearly the same treatment.

The judge said, "Do not do it again," and threw out my ticket, along with the fine, after telling my attorney he owed him a beer. Not that I was ungrateful for the lackluster handling of the law, but I was in shock that the justice system was nothing more than a series of deals, arrangements if you will, agreed to by those working within in it and disseminated to those who do not. In other words, it was a business.

In the same vein, the political system in America is nothing more than a business. In fact, the federal government is quite possibly the largest corporation on the planet, though rather than being lean, it operates at maximum inefficiency. Once you recognize this truth, the veil over Washington can be lifted for you as it was for me so many years ago. Why do you think it is that so many people work for the government? Think about what the unemployment rate would really look like if the federal government was to shut down. Now think about how your tax dollars employ those leeches and ponder on the government shutdown of only a few years ago. Do you not wish that we had grown a proverbial pair and simply let it happen? We do not need the government to be running in such a massive, over-inflated capacity and the fact that we do, in my opinion, truly proves just how lackadaisical we as a people have become.

Can you tell me what would happen to any business which operated at this level of inefficiency within the private sector? Any business, not just a large corporation, but even the local lemonade stand down the road, ran by those annoying little girls that flash their adorable eyes at you in hopes you will break down and pay the 25 cents. I do not want lemonade, please stop asking me! It only makes me feel bad to continually reject the overly sweet cancer liquid! Sorry for that, I think I went off on a tangent, but seriously, can anyone answer my question? Anyone? Bueller?

Any business operating at this level of inefficiency would go out of business. They would be shut down within six months and the reason is simple economics. Let us expand on this subject for a moment and perhaps we can all come to a better understanding of why our government is continually demanding higher taxes and yet seems to be incapable of actually producing anything of value.

Have you ever walked into a Chic-Fil-A at high noon? The place is a complete mad house and frankly, I am often a part of the chaos. Those chicken sandwiches are delicious and the service is not only fantastic but very fast. This means that the food service is efficient, right? Would you categorize Chic-Fil-A as an efficient business? Well, how about the fact that during the lunch rush, there is a multitude of people working there. Have you ever taken notice of the number of people behind the counter during lunch time? It is like a small army and they need it, in order that they can maintain their service quality and speed.

You see, it is all about supply and demand, simple economics. With more demand, you require more supply, otherwise, you will become obsolete. Chic-Fil-A understands this and therefore, due to the fact that there is a demand for fast, efficient, and quality service every day around lunch time, they provide a higher supply of employees to take care of the customers as well as a higher supply of chicken sandwiches to fill their demand.

Now imagine the Shoney's sitting across the road from that same Chic-Fil-A, at the very same time during the day. Can you see it in your mind? Did you immediately picture an empty parking lot? How many employees do you think are working in there at lunch time? Let me answer that question for you rather generically; not even close to the amount which can be found in Chic-Fil-A. There are fewer customers, meaning less demand, which means the company is supplying less food and workforce. Naturally, given the fact that the rent cost on the building is similar to that of the Chic-Fil-A, they will also most likely be out of business long before their adversaries across the road; but can you imagine the accelerated timeline of that ultimate demise if they were employing the same number of people every day as Chic-Fil-A? They would be closed down inside of a week! An increase in supply with no demand equals debt and as anyone reading this who went to college will know, debt without repayment can only be maintained for a limited amount of time. The pied piper always comes to collect, as the saying goes.

My fellow Americans, the pied piper is coming to collect on the national debt of the United States. We are like a Shoney's that is operating with an overinflated workforce but lacks any product. Why is there no product? Because we have a budget which allows room for payouts to those who don't contribute back to the system. Think about it. We give handouts to illegal aliens, we send care packages in the form of monetary support to most of the world, we give more money to U.N. agendas than any other country, we pay our government employees ridiculous amounts of money with no performance accountability, and we give welfare to basically anyone who shows up to receive it. This is why we want a wall on the southern border, not because we do not believe in the "dreamers," as the left would have you believe, but because the economy is in the toilet. This is why we want to drain the swamp and why we need Donald Trump to renegotiate our trade deals and foreign agreements. Not because we do not want to be a part of the world, hold hands, and sing Michael Jackson songs all day, but because the globalists in the government have taken over our national interests, stuffed their pockets with our hard earned money, directed us into foreign agendas which are not in our best interests, and all the while are sucking us dry. How can I say it in layman's terms? We are going broke, belly-up, we have screwed the pooch, is any of this making sense to you?

Let me give you some facts. Steve Forbes wrote an incredibly revealing article back in 2014 at Forbes.com entitled, "U.S. Gives Financial Aid to 96% of All Countries." I will only paraphrase what he said, but I think the title is relatively self-explanatory. He wrote that in 2012, the United States was the world's largest donor, paying out something to the tune of 48 billion dollars. We gave more than 30 billion in financial assistance and more than 17 billion to foreign militaries. The U.N. has 193 members and evidently, we contributed money and aid to 184 of them. Can you believe that!?

This is only a small representation of what your tax dollars are going to, rather than being spent to rebuild the crumbling infrastructure throughout the country. In addition to this, of the top six countries we have contributed money to, five contain a Muslim majority! Yet Linda Sarsour has the nerve to stand up in front of the largest gathering of Muslims in our country and call for Jihad against Donald Trump, saying he is an imperialist, a bigot, and touts the recklessness and moral ineptitude of America.

If the rest of the world hates us so much, then why are we providing all of this money to so many countries? If we have so many financial problems here at home, then why are we giving out 50 billion dollars annually to other countries? If China is the largest owner of U.S. debt, then why do we send them financial aid at all? Did I just blow your mind a little? Can you imagine how much better off we would be if we could convince Congress to appropriate those funds to homegrown needs? They could continue getting rich and rebuild the country at the same time! Nevertheless, we, the middle class, suffer while Congress passes swollen budgets and takes long, undeserved vacations. I ask you, how could any real American abide this sort of behavior? I will attempt to answer that question.

I have had many people ask me what I mean when I use the term "globalist" to describe the congressmen and women who claim to represent us. This, my friends, is what I mean. A government entity which refuses to see the needs at home and yet continues to provide funding to foreign interests is a globalist. We have been overrun by them, taken over, and guess what? These same globalists are the ones in bed with the propaganda machine chugging along behind the media, programming you to believe that we owe this money to the world and that our prosperity is not our own. It is a lie, a falsehood propagated to convince Americans that the unmistakable, apprehensible crime taking place right now in Washington is normal and that the agenda to bankrupt our country is merely a conspiracy theory. That being said, let us take a closer look at this so called conspiracy and the people who manage it.

Do you know why the national debt limit has been increased over 100 times since 1940? Wait, were you not aware of that fact? Look it up in politifact.com, you can see it for yourself. Remember when Obama made the statement, "... raising the debt ceiling does not allow Congress to spend more money. It simply gives our country the ability to pay the bills Congress has already racked up."? As absurd as that sounds, he is correct, it was just simply a terrible pitch for asking Congress to sign on to yet another debt increase. I mean, how stupid do you have to be to give someone money who says to you, "I need a loan to pay back someone else who just gave me a loan?" Would you give money to that person? Do not lie, because we gave Obama the money when he said the same thing.

This is the inherent problem with our government bureaucracy as it stands now. The government continues to spend more money each year than they make and just to be clear, there is only one way for it to make any money, by collecting taxes. Why do you think your taxes continue to increase? For that matter, why do you think tax reductions are the only leverage politicians have to be able to swindle your vote every two years? Do you ever pay any attention to the headlines that say, "Congress collects record high taxes?" You should, because therein lies the real accountability we as Americans have in our government.

I will reference back to a headline from the freebeacon.com in 2016 which read, "$1.48 Trillion: Government Collects Record-High Taxes in First Half of FY 2016." In it, they continued by saying that though the collection was a record, the government still ran a deficit totaling more than 450 billion dollars. Do you think that fact has stifled any expenditures by the Congress? Trump is still trying to convince them to pass his tax reforms and yet the left is diverting more and more into this Russia garbage, which I can assure you is nothing more than a diversion created to shift your focus away from the real problems we face. Our nation's economy is in full on crisis mode and here is the real conspiracy: the debt is spiraling out of control, Trump has a fantastic plan to balance the budget and wants to work with Congress to fix it, but Congress wants to bankrupt the country.

What else could possibly explain record tax collections alongside the largest deficit in our history? How can we be bringing in that much money and continue building that much debt? Why would any responsible legislator pass a budget which spends more than we bring in? The answer is right there for us all to see. It is not a difficult concept, our legislative branch is run by politicians, not businessmen and women. Politicians are decorated used-car salesmen who say anything to take your money. They will sell you a cardboard truck and call it a tank, just to make the commission. Card-sharks ladies and gentlemen and the game is politics; a business, which has incredible power over your daily life, but which is run by poker players that have already stacked the deck against your favor.

This is the reason that we elected Donald Trump to drain the swamp, because we have grown tired of these career, bureaucrat politicians running our lives, taking our money, and giving us nothing in return. It is time to install normal business ethics and guidelines into this extremely inefficient corporation we call a government, but that would mean an end to the gravy train operated by our representatives. As you can see from the war which has ensued against Trumps administration, the establishment wants nothing to do with it. However, before we continue with that topic any further, let me take you back to the conspiracy at hand because I think it is important to outline the budget crisis facing the near-future generations of America.

There is a creature which lives in the bowels of our nation, bred with the sole purpose of taking down our republic from within. It is not King Kong or the Loch-Ness Monster, in fact, it is not a literal living creature, but instead a festering, disgusting being of administration. Its name is the Federal Reserve. You may have heard of it, the private bank which has complete control over our currency. You know, the one which masks itself as a government body but can be more accurately described as a member of the global network of central banks, controlled from London, which has sought to consolidate and influence the flow of money worldwide for decades.

The Federal Reserve is in no way federal, and while the President appoints a head of the Federal Reserve, this is merely an exercise in deceit. The Wall Street bankers, from which the head of the Fed is often chosen, are so deeply rooted in the global banking scheme, the President could, in reality, chose any of them and the outcome would be the same: Managing the economy to suit the needs of the bankers. This is unfortunately too general, however, let me speak a bit more technical and we can examine the facts.

The Federal Reserve is the bank which controls the money supply in America. It is owned privately by European as well as American families and it is in business merely to loan money to the United States and profit from the interest which it charges. As fancy as it may sound, the fact is that it is nothing more than a bejeweled loan shark. Tell me, have you ever taken notice of the statement at the top of your printed dollars, "Federal Reserve Note?" What do you think that means exactly? That is right, it is not real money, but rather a "note." In fact, it is much more akin to an "I owe you" than actual money, nevertheless, our entire economic system operates on it.

The real treat of the Fed is that it is publicly subsidized, meaning that any losses they incur off of their loans to American banks will be covered by the government, a.k.a, your tax dollars. Remember when Obama bailed the banks out, saying that they were "too big to fail?" Remember thinking to yourself that "this is absurd, if they cannot manage their finances well enough, then they do not deserve to be in business?" Well, guess what? We, the American people via Congress, allow this tremendously inefficient business known as the Fed to continually mismanage our money supply on an annual basis and, as I mentioned previously, there is no accountability whatsoever! The Fed has never been audited by the U.S. government and therefore, they can do whatever they want. In fact, as Janet Yellen said herself, "I want to be completely clear that I strongly oppose Audit the Fed. Audit the Fed is a bill that would politicize monetary policy and it would bring short-term political pressure to bear on the Fed." In other words, "step off, I do what I want and the American people are not allowed to govern me."

Imagine the cojones on this woman! She stands directly in the face of the government which legislates for we the people and creates the budget year after year and tells them to directly kiss her ass! Amazing, but yet, this is the situation we find ourselves in. A private organization controls our wealth and manages it for personal gain, but lies to our face and says that they are the only ones who can manage the economy, due to the overly complex algorithms required which the average person would simply not understand. In case you were not aware of the quote by our founding father Thomas Jefferson, let me remind you of his well-educated words:

> "I believe that banking institutions are more dangerous to our liberties than standing armies. If the American people ever allow private banks to control the issue of their currency, first by inflation, then by deflation, the banks and corporations that will grow up around [the banks] will deprive the people of all property until their children wake-up homeless on the continent their

fathers conquered. The issuing power should be taken from the banks and restored to the people, to whom it properly belongs."

A true profit ahead of his time and yet, we have become so arrogant and apathetic that we have instituted the very thing our founding fathers warned us against. Now, I do not want to stray too far from the explanation, so I will ask a simple question. Have you ever wondered why we need to continue raising the debt limit? I know I have and the answer is obvious once you understand the way the Federal Reserve works.

The Fed loans money to the government, or banks, or really whoever asks for it, with interest. This is not the end to the conspiracy, however, the developers of the Reserve knew they would need a way to ensure that the interest would actually be collected. After all, the Fed loans money out to banks for free. Therefore, if they could not actually collect on the interest, they would have then driven themselves out of business long ago. Imagine where our government would be if these people were not crooks and instead ran our country for the good of the people.

They, therefore, instituted another massive bureaucracy which to this day remains an unconstitutional infringement on our rights as U.S. citizens: The Internal Revenue Service. Yes indeed, the IRS is a tax collection service which takes your money and pays the interest on the bonds to the Fed. To make it more direct, your taxes only pay the interest on the debt our government has incurred from the Fed. In order to keep paying those bills Congress has already racked up, as Obama said, they have to then borrow more money from the Federal Reserve, which in turn causes more debt, which is paid by then raising your taxes. I think they call this a vicious circle, and it is an incredibly clever circle manufactured by extremely intelligent treasure pirates who have been, since the early 1900's, defrauding the entire population of America year after year.

I am sure you are asking yourself, "Why on Earth would we have ever instituted such a prison of finance into our government?" To be honest, the idea that was presented to the Congress sounded good, in fact, had it been given the proper oversight and been used the way in which it was originally pitched, the Fed could have been helpful. Nevertheless, it was only sold as a bag of goods in order to bring down the greatest wealth ever generated from a free society in world history.

The European bankers, which we won our independence from in 1776 (Remember the Boston Tea Party, Taxation without representation, all of that?), never ceased in their attempt to once again enslave the colonists who founded our great nation. Though it took a few hundred years, with the installation of the IRS and the Federal Reserve Act in 1913, the Rothschild's, the Rockefellers, and so many others had finally found their way into a position of total control over the American prosperity machine.

The idea was to establish an elastic supply of money, meaning that based on variable economic activity within the country, there would be a body of governance over the flow of currency which could expand and then subsequently shrink the amount of money in circulation. This would, in theory, allow stock prices and the financial state of the country to remain static in an ever changing, worldwide economic environment.

The problem was, instead of following this plan, the Fed proceeded to create a pseudo-science out of inflating and deflating the economy to increase their own profit margin at the relative expense of the American taxpayer. In the wake of it all, the dollar has been consequently devalued nearly 95% since 1913 and the Federal Reserve now holds the government hostage, leveraging interest rates to maintain their unconstitutional debt collection racket.

Let us examine the "Roaring twenties." Remember reading about them in The Great Gatsby? That did not take place simply because we were lucky. It was engineered by the central bankers. The Fed, newly established in the U.S., artificially inflated the economy, loaning out tons of money. The American people were oblivious to the reality of the situation and spent to their heart's desire. Surely you have heard the phrase, "money does not grow on trees," from you parents? Well, the next time someone says that to you, you can tell them that "actually, it comes out of thin air from the Federal Reserve."

This was, in fact, the case in the 1920's and, with all of the loans safely spent by the public, the Fed called in on them in 1929 which, if you are a fan of history you are aware, crashed the stock market. This led to the government collecting all gold in 1934 in exchange for Federal Reserve Notes and thus, the real wealth in America had disappeared and the fraud of the Federal Reserve had begun. Ever since then, the American public has been indebted to the Fed and anyone else willing to buy up the bonds held by the central bank, which is why you often hear that "China owns most of our debt." It is not a conspiracy, it is real, actual fact and as I said earlier, the pied piper is coming to collect his due.

Now, turning our focus to the Presidency, the last President to legitimately balance the national budget was Andrew Jackson. As unbelievable as that sounds, it is true. He put a stop to the second national bank, which preceded the Federal Reserve and for the first and only time in our nation's history, he paid off the national debt. This was in 1835 and ironically, that same year, there was an attempt made on his life. Coincidence? I think not. The next President who went to battle with the Fed was John F. Kennedy. He, in my opinion, was the last real President we had before Donald Trump. Kennedy mimicked Abraham Lincoln's actions from the 1800's by authorizing the U.S. treasury to issue its own money, outside of the control of the international banking cartel in 1963. Did you read that year closely? Because in case you do not pay attention in history class, later in 1963, Kennedy was shot in Texas; Coincidence? I think not.

My friends, I have given this short history lesson to paint a picture for you, a picture of the business of politics. Ever since Kennedy was assassinated, a precedent has been set for the President of the United States that you simply do not mess with the Fed. No President until Trump has ever talked about auditing the Fed and no President has ever locked horns with the bankers. Can you understand now why Obama would do something so stupid as to bail out the banks? Why he would justify it by saying they were "too big to fail?"

Career politicians may be smart and are most certainly clever, but they lack any real business IQ. This is why those who do understand business and who wish to use that knowledge to influence government, like George Soros for example, have spent their money leveraging politicians with blackmail and hiring lobbyists to apply political pressure with the aim of protecting their interests. Career politicians then subsequently use pay to play schemes, developed in Washington, in order to garner massive campaign budgets, which ultimately enable them to monopolize seats in Congress.

Due to these circumstances, the task may seem daunting, but it is now more important than ever: We must take back the government from the cronies. Not by force, not yet anyway, but through a smart, business aptitude which is lacking in the minds of our representatives. People who are able to understand the level of corruption that exists in Washington, where it is derived from, and how to effectively break it down by trimming the fat and balancing the budget.

For this reason, to me anyway, Donald Trump was the clear choice for President in 2016. A successful businessman who not only harbored the celebrity appeal and funding to win an election against Hilary Clinton, but who possesses the predisposition for business which we can use to our advantage while making America great again.

We are destitute, we are broken, but we are not yet completely destroyed and we can, therefore, cut the waste, balance the budget, and put our people back to work in the private sector; generating tax contributors, instead of tax receivers. The establishment has gotten rich off of the rotten deals which are filtering money out of the country and further indebting us to the bankers. They are therefore in a full on war against Donald Trump, fabricating lies and bombarding his administration with any ammunition they can find to sidetrack his agenda. They do not want to interrupt the status quo, they do not want the leverage on them to be surfaced, but we must see past these falsehoods and vote them out of a job!

Maxine Watters does not even live in her district. She lives in a high end, gated neighborhood, in a mansion which occupies a city block. Where did that money come from? How can she claim to represent the lower class when she has profited off of their indentured servitude. Nancy Pelosi can barely speak, but she remains in office long past her prime, bumbling around on television so that she can continue pocketing your tax dollars. Why is the media worried about Trump's tax returns and not Pelosi's? Bernie Sanders calls the corporations the enemy, but he bought a mansion after his failed campaign and his wife is under investigation for defrauding a university. Did he run for President to steal votes from the Republicans in exchange for personal donations?

I could go on and on, but I think the point is clear. These are the real questions which should be investigated by the media in an era when the entirety of their focus is on bringing down Donald Trump. The swamp is like a cornered rat, dangerous, but we must stand strong against the real oppressors living in Washington, stealing your tax money and funding everything but the well-being of this county. We must reject the propaganda machine which says that we do not deserve our wealth, but the U.N. does. People of America, I say to you, readers of this book, let us put our support and trust in the man we elected. Let us allow him to drain this swamp, and get down to the nitty, gritty, business of politics.

Chapter Four

Trumping Imperialism

Donald Trump has been relentlessly accused of being an imperialist. In the case that it does not go without saying, he has been given such a designation with nigh a shred of evidence. Naturally, the name calling does not end there, seeing that he has also been accused of being a fascist, a bigot, and a thug as well, but I think it is important to take these analogies and break them down for the reading audience, so that you can once again see the misrepresentation of the mainstream media for yourself.

Often, a tactic of the democratic left is to superimpose their own iniquities onto the opposition, in an attempt to cover their tracks and the attacks on Trump are certainly not exceptions. For me, however, the accusation of Imperialism is particularly interesting, given the fact that American imperialism has been continuous and unremitting in nearly every presidential administration since 1907 when Theodore Roosevelt sent his "Great White Fleet" to sail around the world in a show of naval force.

The answer to the question, "When did America become an empire?" is most definitely a topic for a totally different book, in fact, perhaps I will make this my focus for the sequel. Nevertheless, when discussing the idea of Trump as an imperialist, it is extremely important to consider the historical facts in order to create a plausible frame of reference. Regardless of when America became an imperialistic nation, the fact is that today, we are one. More importantly, it did not begin with Trump and it most certainly did not end with Barack Obama.

Is that a hard pill to swallow? Were you operating under the assumption that we were always the good guys and our "meddling" in foreign affairs was simply a means to spread the loving effects of freedom? Team America was a more relevant film than you may be willing to admit, considering our role as the police force of the world is derived from an overall submission of our military, by our own government, to the harassment and intimidation of the United Nations. Prosperity may have built the structure of wealth and influence we enjoy as a country, but the freedom to do what you want can also lead to imposing your will on those who do not welcome it, especially when your foreign policy is governed by an outside, unelected political authority.

Let us begin with a simple definition, just in case you have no idea what I am talking about. What is imperialism? Webster's dictionary defines it as "the policy, practice, or advocacy of extending the power and dominion of a nation especially by direct territorial acquisitions or by gaining indirect control over the political or economic life of other areas." In other words, it is the act of gaining political power over a different nation using either direct or indirect force, which could be anything from military intervention to economic sanctions. Does that sound familiar?

Let me ask you a question, how would you categorize the ongoing conflict we have in the Middle East? Do you really believe that either Bush or Obama planned on ending the war on terror anytime soon? Do you not think an end to the war could have been decisive had anyone in Washington felt it was not more profitable to let it continue than to pull out all of the troops and resources? Obama said he would end the war in Iraq and bring all of the troop's home. In fact, he said on the campaign trail in 2012 that he himself had ended the war.

If I remember correctly, he said that he "said what he meant," and he "ended it." Remember that? In that case, perhaps you also remember two years later, sometime around August of 2014, when he explained that we would be renewing air strikes in Iraq. When questioned by the media as to whether or not he wished he had left troops in place, Obama blamed the dial down of resources on the democratically elected government in Iraq, implemented by George W. Bush. Obama claimed that he did not decide to remove our troops, they were simply no longer invited by the Iraqi government.

Insane, right? Barack Obama often blamed his terrible foreign policy failures on Bush, but then willingly accepted peace awards and claimed to be the great peace maker when the cameras were turned on. To be clear, Donald Trump has made statements that Iraq is a mess and that we should have left the troops in position for stability. Not because he agreed with our actions in the region, but because once the decision had been made to go in, leaving it like Obama did only caused more instability, more violence, and ensured the overall demise of the government we helped install.

Trump was against the war from the start. Look it up on factcheck.org, even they, a left-wing organization, can find no evidence of Trump supporting the war. They could find, however, a conversation Trump had with Neil Cavuto in 2003, where he said that the economy was more important than the War in Iraq and that he wished we could spend the money on New York City instead of overseas.

Here's the point, our foreign policy has been, for some time, more focused on causing instability than creating lasting peace. You know the old additive, "be a blessing, not a burden?" Evidently, our lawmakers were not subjected to such good advice as children and the result is obvious.

Indeed, September 11th was an immense tragedy, one that is absolutely beyond definition or categorization. Nevertheless, the fact remains that it was perpetrated by a majority of Saudi Arabians instead of Afghans, which at the very least serves to argue that we attacked the wrong country. I do not wish to get into so much detail on this particular topic, but why would Bush abide such a charade when the retaliation, which later led to the founding of the War on Terror, most likely assisted with the spread of Jihad and can arguably be labeled as a worse incident than the actual bombing of the Twin Towers?

I would like to examine some examples of our more recent foreign policies to see if they were truly stabilizing in nature, or rather imperialistic. Because in my opinion, the left referring to Donald Trump as an imperialist is something of the pot calling the kettle black. From my chair, Trump is serving to break with the status quo and shift our focus from expanding our interests abroad, to securing our infrastructure and financial situation domestically.

Imagine if we had spent the last sixteen years bolstering our security at home, rather than attacking the Middle East. Do you not believe that we would be in a more comfortable and self-assured state of affairs than we find ourselves today? I mean, the main reason we went to war after

September 11th was due to the fact that suddenly, we were made aware of the weakness within our national security. "Shock and Awe" was due more to the shock we received when a commercial airliner ran into our tallest skyscraper and the awe that the superstructure of power we had been building since World War II was actually, unbelievably, vulnerable.

Now, there is no doubt that retaliation was a necessary evil at that stage, though at this point we can debate whether or not it was an "inside job." Regardless, once the retribution had been achieved, why did we not focus our budget on restoring our republic, rather than enslaving it with the TSA and the ever-omniscient NSA? A nearly immeasurable amount of money has been loaned from the Federal Reserve to build the massive network of infiltration into our daily lives, known as the National Security Agency, under the guise of protecting our freedoms. As I am sure you are aware, the realistic effect is the exact opposite, as the only way for the federal government to spy on the American people is to specifically infringe upon our inalienable rights. Yet, the operation continues to this day, expanded on a massive scale under Obama and harboring no end in sight from the refusal of Congress to make any steps toward cutting one iota of its funding.

As a matter of fact, Obama was caught, along with his national security advisor, Susan Rice, using the intelligence services to spy on thousands of Americans during the 2016 Presidential campaign, the majority of which were conservatives. Among those masses was one group of particular interest. Can you guess to which group I am referring? That is right, the Trump presidential campaign.

It is not so hard to believe, is it? How else do you think all of these leaks during the first year of Trump's administration have been possible? How else do you think the media acquired knowledge of who Jeff Sessions met with or who Jared Kushner was emailing with? Why is it that all of the leaks have become the unrelenting central focus of the MSM, but yet the fact that Obama instigated the collection of the data is history and has yet to lead to any indictments or Congressional hearings? I am of the opinion that once Donald Trump is able to get back on the offensive he will bring these criminals to justice, but until that time, we remain in a war of our own: the info war.

This was, however, merely one of Obama's numerous transgressions while in office, many of which dealt more with foreign affairs. It is these calamities which I now want to spotlight and further consider their imperialistic nature. To begin with, do you remember that one of Obama's first actions in office was to expand the war in Afghanistan? Most likely you have forgotten that though his Presidential campaign was littered with claims of ending the war in Iraq, this was merely a ploy to gain the support of the democratic majority (more than 50% of which were opposed to an expansion of the war in the Middle East). No, Barack Obama was most assuredly an agent of Wall Street and the military industrial complex, no different than his predecessor George W. Bush.

It is my opinion that Obama never had any intention of putting an end to our intervention in the Middle East, although with this topic, he proved his mastery of deception. To the public, he presented a weak front that wavered on the topic of war in order to emphasize an internal moral struggle. Behind closed doors told a different story as he was in reality, merely a war monger identical to the new world order cronies preceding him.

Obama requested somewhere close to 20 billion dollars from Congress to both trains an Afghan army and fund additional resources for U.S. troops. That meant boots on the ground and given the timeline he presented of seven years, it also suggested no end in sight for our involvement in the destabilization campaign in the Middle East. I think it is relatively obvious at this point that the conflict in the region was in no way intended to garner peace. After all, peace allows for a stable government, which translates to the ability for self-governance.

While our government may peddle talking points to the media which insinuate our interest in peace for the Middle East, the truth is radically different. With chaos, we can impose our will, meaning control over the infamous oil reserves as well as the ever-controversial poppy fields, along with any other natural resources we may see fit to collect. Much like the colonial rule of Britain over the new world before the founding of America, we have sat on top of Iraq and Afghanistan, instigating variability and ultimately reaping the rewards for ourselves.

Naturally, the resources are not the only benefit of a never-ending conflict. I mentioned that Obama was an agent of Wall Street; what do you think the term "war-time profiteering," really means? I am here to tell you that when there is war, the corporations who build the weapons, manufacture the ammunition and the tanks, provide the armor, package the rations, build the jets, build the engines for the jets, and the logistics companies who coordinate the transportation for all of these items stand to benefit from the business of war.

Oh, I apologize, you were assuming that my point was to only insinuate the existence of a political business? War is just as much of a dirty industry as politics and for thousands of years, the 1% have managed to walk hand in hand with both sides. It is unfortunate that the U.S. has been involved in such an appalling strain on world events, but the only question now is, what shall we do about it going forward?

The expansion of the Iraq war was one of his first actions, but the second exploit of Obama was to expand the conflict in Pakistan. This can be labeled as an unofficial war, as it was never actually voted on by Congress. In fact, it might come as a surprise to find out that the last time Congress actually voted to declare war on another country was in 1941. If you will remember your U.S. history for a moment, perhaps you can recall that the Constitution gives the power to declare war solely to the Congress, not to the President. Yet the White House, the Pentagon, and the State Department have unilaterally decided to carry out military actions against scores of other countries since World War II and our loving, crony, career politicians have voted to pay for it in lock step, like tin soldiers receiving their wound-up orders. Obama chose to expand these so called "military actions" in Pakistan, which was made up mostly of drone strikes but also included some raids and undercover CIA operations as well.

Obama, like every other American President in the last century, was more concerned about expanding our power and authority over the rest of the world in order to further secure the empire which has been built since the 1940's. Sounds a bit like an imperialist, does it not? The problem is, while that empire may have a "Made in America" sticker on it, it is not American by any stretch of the imagination. This is, after all, yet another reason we elected Donald Trump, right? Because we are tired of meddling in foreign affairs and want to re-establish our interest in America first?

It was not just a clever campaign slogan, the phrase, "America first," actually means something. It means we want to put our hard-earned money into securing the borders that Obama abolished and cut back on the aid to foreign governments who hate us. It means we want to rebuild our own infrastructure, rather than destabilizing Middle Eastern governments and installing the Muslim Brotherhood in order to appease the United Nations. Woah. Hold on a second, I want to make sure you really let that one sink in, because I am about to pour some truth into the mix, specifically for your reading pleasures.

I believe that the expansion of the American empire was always intended as a vehicle for the establishment and governance of the New World Order. After all, the United Nations has no official military. Therefore, what better political entity than the one which retains the largest standing army on the planet to centralize control of the world indirectly through a campaign of destabilization?

Can you think of another reason why so many American Presidents would willingly bankrupt the United States by paying to build up other countries after they created the damage in the first place? Can you think of any other reason why Obama would intentionally bring in tens of thousands of refugees from South America and offer them a free ride, courtesy of our tax dollars? How about a different reason why Germany would accept tens of thousands of Muslim refugees from Syria? Are these not all egregious acts of treason? Let me ask you this, what exactly did you think these refugee crises were all about? Did you not find it curious that they were happening at the same time?

Let us take a closer look at this topic. The United States played a major role in creating the refugee crisis in Europe when Obama failed to temper the debacle known as the Arab Spring. Why then would Germany, France, Italy, and other European countries be willing to accept the refugees, rather than insisting that the U.S. take them or at the very least, pay for them? Unless of course, it was a plan from the U.N., carefully crafted and carried out by its submissive members complicit in the founding of the New World Order. Not convinced? Then let us go one step further.

Obama himself caused the refugee crisis in South America and Mexico when he and Eric Holder ran the Fast and Furious armament scandal with the drug cartels. How can there be any spin job which justifies this as anything more than an attempt to depose the legitimate government in Mexico? Why did Congress not investigate this incredible criminal activity and put Holder and Obama in a maximum security prison? It does not make sense. That is of course unless it was a plan from the U.N., carefully crafted and carried out by the submissive U.S. government, which under Obama, was most definitely complicit in the founding of the New World Order. Are you starting to understand my point?

Now, the Arab Spring is a key element to understanding the imperialist Obama agenda, but it is also paramount in understanding the difference between what Obama and his predecessors sought to achieve and what Trump is now attempting to reverse. However, before I can lay out that explanation, it is vital that you the reader have a full understanding of what exactly the New World Order is. Because make no mistake about it, this entity is very real and it is constantly working to both undermine your way of life and radically alter the open and unbound freedom both you and I enjoy.

For decades the NWO has been seen as nothing more than a conspiracy theory, but as they become more public with their attempts at total monopolization of worldwide power, there can no longer be any denial of what the Order is and what it stands for. Again I will ask the question, does it make sense to you that Congress has continually funded an undeclared War on Terror? Can you find a logical reason that the liberal left refuses to see the benefit of restricting immigration from dangerously unstable countries harboring Muslim terrorists? It may be a hard concept to fathom, but these are not random occurrences and Washington is not struggling with the morality of their decisions. American imperialism is only a small part of a very large, well-engineered plan to rule the world and double cross the citizens of the U.S. in the process.

Let us then examine the New World Order. It is indeed a conspiracy, but not in the sense that it is a fabricated myth made up by crack pots. It is, in fact, an actual, criminal plan to violate the inherent rights of humanity, kept in secret by those enmeshed in its creation. I am sure you have heard as much as I have the globalists on the left, take Bill Gates, for example, touting the idea of overpopulation on the Earth. Now there is a real conspiracy theory made up by crack pots, in case you were wondering what it actually looks and sounds like. Not that I want to stray too far from the main topic here, but I feel it is my duty as the author to make this point. There are indeed overpopulated cities on our planet, Los Angeles is full to the brim and starting to spill over. However, the Earth is nowhere even close to being overpopulated and those who continue to babble on with this disinformation are clearly misinformed. If you do not believe me, take a trip to North Dakota and tell me how many people you see, then come back here and finish reading.

Nevertheless, the idea behind the New World Order is to establish a one world government, in which the 99% are completely dependent on that government and in exchange for goods and services, they perform all of the necessary production to maintain life on Earth. Imagine every science fiction movie you have seen and apply its lessons to real life. You know, movies like the Matrix, Equilibrium, Logan's Run, Blade Runner...shall I go on, or do you get the picture?

This is, in fact, the actual goal of the 1% here on Earth. Is it so hard to believe? They say absolute power corrupts absolutely. Think about how much power the social engineers and globalist, corporate figure heads have managed to acquire for themselves. Now imagine the entire group banding together and attempting to consolidate that power in order to rule the world. Did you think cartoon characters like "the Brain" from "Pinky and the Brain," were simply clever comedic entries to a new generation of art? Did you not ever stop to ponder on the fact that these characters are actually facsimiles of real people, really plotting to take over the world, in real life?

I think you can start to understand how much trouble we are essentially in as a society and also the severe significance of the election of Donald Trump. We do not just need a break from the status quo of the liberal left, we need liberation from a global power that has invaded our government and taken control of our American agenda. The globalists which occupy Washington are the true imperialists, but their vision does not include merely the expansion of the American empire, though that is where it begins. Rather, they seek something much larger, something much more permanent: world domination. Now, I imagine you are wanting further detail of how Obama, the Bush's, and Clinton's agendas are intertwined within the conspiracy of the NWO, so allow me to check off just a few of the elements required by such a worldwide system.

First of all, there would need to be a one world currency. Now, we have already discussed the Federal Reserve and the fact that the flow of money in the United States is all based on thin air. The United States government took the gold from the American people in 1934 using the legislation known as The Gold Reserve Act. This officially outlawed private ownership of gold and forced the U.S. citizens to sell their gold to the Federal Reserve in exchange for Reserve Notes. Once all currency in the U.S. existed only in the form of paper money, the government was able to remove the Gold Standard. In case you do not know, this was a rule which limited the printing of money to a volume which could be physically represented by gold. From then on, the Federal Reserve printed money at will, based on nothing, and their scientific system of economic control over the United States, by way of periodic inflation and deflation, was well established.

The same system of central banking was also created in Europe with the establishment of the European Union. It was not so long ago that all of the European countries maintained their own systems of currency, language, and borders, and with those key elements, they, therefore, were able to maintain sovereignty. Once the EU was in place, the countries of Europe transferred their power to Brussels and everything changed. The flow of money was then dictated through the use of a paper currency known as the Euro, borders were abolished, creating one massive country, and English became the primary language. At this point, the globalist, central bankers were able to create their own legislation and manipulate the economy at will in the same manner that they hold the American government hostage. In other words, check mark, the U.N. is only one step away from a one world currency. I should note that the United Nations is the embodiment of the New World Order. It is what the League of Nations failed to be after World War I, the unelected governing body for world governance which now dictates political agendas to its members (Including the EU, the U.S., China, etc.).

Do you now have a better understanding of why NWO puppets, masquerading as U.S. Presidents, would be so loose with our money? By bankrupting the country domestically in order to fund the empire abroad, they could transfer the power of the United States to the United Nations (a.k.a. The New World Order), in a double cross of the American people who voted for the puppets like Barack Obama in the first place.

Is that too much for you to take in? Let me harken you back to the question of why we spend more money than we bring in? Can you better explain that travesty? Does it not make sense that people smart enough to make their way into public office would simply be following a plan of social engineering, rather than bankrupting the country due to negligence? I refuse to believe that balancing the budget is so difficult. After all, I voted for Donald Trump because he ran on that concept as his campaign platform, but I digress.

There would also need to be centralized control over natural resources with which the NWO could use to leverage governments. Think about it, by nullifying the flow of money using a paper system, natural resources become the only real power maintained by sovereign nations. Shall we revisit the fact that the American empire destabilized the Middle East in order to gain control over its natural resources?

As we previously discussed, oil may not have been the only reason for the War in Iraq and Afghanistan, but it was nevertheless an element of it; do you remember the fact that Joe Biden's son was given a seat on the board of Burisma Holdings? Not to mention, the more recent meddling of the U.S. government in Syria is highly suspect, considering the Russian implications. Obama was the one who drew the red line in Syria in an obvious attempt to instigate a conflict centered on the overthrow of Bashar Al Assad, knowing that the Russians back his administration.

By the way, Trump just negotiated a cease fire between the U.S. and Russia in Syria during the G20. I know that Trump is the consummate deal maker, but do you not think Obama could have done the same thing if he had wanted to? I wonder why, exactly, Obama was so hesitant to make peace and instead continued to inflame tensions with Russia as if it were the Cold War? I think I will break it down for you a little further.

Were you aware that Russia is the largest exporter of oil and natural gas to the European Union? Interesting, is it not? The fact that we discussed previously concerning the mouthwatering neo-cons in Congress and their lust for war with Russia? Again I will ask the question, why do you think Hilary Clinton, John McCain, Lindsey Graham, Barack Obama, and so many others are dead set on war with Putin? Why would they go to such great lengths to destabilize decades of diplomatic relationships, seemingly on purpose? Even to the extent that they would fabricate a false narrative highlighting Putin's collusion with Donald Trump and the hacking of our electoral process in 2016 in order to ensure his election. A storyline that is clearly intended to depose Trump in order to realign their agenda of war with Russia!

It simply does not make sense, unless of course, it was part of a U.N. plan, carefully crafted and carried out by the submissive U.S. government in order to further consolidate worldwide natural resources into the hands of the true imperialists of our time. Perhaps that was too fast, let me spell it out for you: check mark, the fight to control the natural resources of the world is well under way. Is this sounding more believable to you? I tell you what, how about one more.

The New World Order would require a mass distraction for the population. One that would ensure the silence of any dissenters and serve to clear the path for their agenda's implementation with a minimum amount of resistance. Makes sense, right? Well, what better distraction than religion? I mean, they gave the cultural and social division a try, but that clearly backfired. Humanity, at least in my opinion, wants peace, we want to get along and evolve. We desire brotherhood and therefore, even in the case of unlimited funding for groups like Black Lives Matter to go out and instigate violence, the majority of the human race will "rise above it," when it comes to racial tension; just like in feel good movies the likes of Remember the Titans and Cool Runnings.

By contrast, when it comes to religion, there is just something about the subject which never ceases to arouse the deepest of emotions. Enter the one world religion, a system intended to occupy the hearts and minds of the populace, while world governance removes all physical elements of freedom from around them. Now, I do not claim to know as fact which religion the NWO has chosen for this task. Some will argue that ultimately science will become the culprit, but I choose to believe it is something more tangible in the here and now. Of course, all of the major religions in our history have spread by force one way or the other, you can find the stories in any encyclopedia.

With that being said, there is only one religion coming to the forefront today which is seemingly being given the green light by the globalists to run amuck and wreak havoc on the world. Only one religion which has established itself as a sovereign state and claims responsibility for every major terror attack we have seen for the past decade. One that treats its women like slaves, throws gays off the tops of buildings and immigrates to other countries demanding the adoption of their Sharia law. You guessed it, as controversial as it may be, the religion I am referring to is radical Islam.

While Obama may have refused to use that label in speeches in order to appease his fellow Muslims, Donald Trump realizes the danger the Islamic State poses to the Western World. While Europe may be willing to bow down and tell its citizens to get used to terror attacks as they are simply a part of everyday life, Trump understands how to put an end to the violence: by smashing the enemy, cutting off their funding, and refusing to accept the "refugees" unless they are willing to prove their interest in cultural adaptation. My friends, the New World Order is installing an agenda right before our very eyes to destroy all other forms of religion, ordain Islam as the new credence, and either force you to submit or remove the ones who do not from the chess board. It may sound harsh, but now that we have come full circle, I think we can safely examine the facts.

Take a look at the Catholic Church being brought down from within, infiltrated for years by pedophiles and now revelations are destroying any credibility they have left. Do you believe it to be a coincidence that gay orgies within the Vatican are taking place at the same time Muslim refugees stand to become the majority in German cities? On the other hand, look at what has happened to Christianity in the past few decades. Army officer's court marshaled for having a bible on their desk, the Ten Commandments taken off of the court houses, children being punished for praying in school. Tell me, when was the last time you saw a "see you at the flag pole" event in your kid's school? You know, where the kids encircle the flag pole and pray? These actions have been removed in the name of fairness and as an attempt to create "safe-spaces" for those who may be offended.

I ask you, what about the wearing of the Hijab or Burka in public? What if that offends me? Do you think anyone would dare ask that question or even move to create a law which bans such attire from the public? It is, after all, a symbol of female slavery. Is that not sexist? Regardless, I see traditional Muslim outfits being worn more and more by actors in television commercials and models on billboards. Does that seem fair to you?

Keeping all of this controversy in mind, I want to turn your attention to the Arab Spring. This was a situation in which Obama was backing rebel factions in Muslim majority countries like Libya, Egypt, and Syria. The idea was that if we armed these factions and gave them training and funding, we could depose the tyrants in the Middle East and oversee democratic elections to install governments ran by the people. Rather than attempting to negotiate peace with the governments, as Trump has recently done, Obama thought overthrowing them indirectly would be a better conduit for stabilization. Using political power to gain indirect control over a region is the definition of imperialism, is it not?

Nevertheless, as you are most likely aware this was, at best, a ghastly scheme and one which has rebounded in a magnificent way, evidenced by the refugee crisis in Europe. Do not get me wrong, Obama was successful in this endeavor, as with the one exception of Syria, the world watched while the people of Egypt and Libya overthrew the autocrats Muammar Gaddafi and Hosni Mubarak. The problem was the fact that the replacements were far worse.

The people of Egypt "elected" Mohammed Morsi, who just happened to be a member of the Muslim brotherhood. Just to be sure we are clear, the Brotherhood has on multiple occasions pledged to destroy the United States and invade and annihilate Jerusalem. Can you imagine then, why Obama would not only be helpful in the establishment of his administration but would embrace him upon their meeting like an old friend and agree to provide him with American F-16 jet fighters? This is a man who, immediately after his election, abolished the Egyptian constitution, which had just been put in place, instituted torture chambers, and justified the silencing of journalists and the judicial system by claiming they were critical of Allah. Sounds like something we should be proud to have been a part of, do you not think?

The real question is, did Obama intend on handing control of Egypt over to the radical Muslims? It seems the alternative would suggest that he is incredibly incompetent, either way, the situation gave a legitimate reason to members of Congress to ask for his resignation, unlike their current reasoning to request Trump's. Egypt was however not the worst of the Arab Spring, considering that Libya is currently a literal hell hole.

The United Nations have backed a unity government led by Mahmoud Jibril and the people have accepted it. Nevertheless, more than 2,000 militants are active in the country and several of them occupy and exercise control over some key areas. IS has a stronghold over the coastline surrounding the city of Sirte, Al-Qaeda controls Derna, and an extremely dangerous group known as Ansar-al-Sharia occupy Benghazi. If you will remember, that was the city in which our consulate was attacked and the ambassador Chris Stevens was murdered, yet another debacle under the imperialist known as Obama.

After the destabilization campaign blew up in our face and Obama made the United States the laughing stock of the world, did Congress request his resignation? Did they move to depose him using the 25th amendment to the Constitution, stating that he was unfit for duty? No? Then let me ask this question, why do you think that is? How could it make sense that Congress would allow him to get away with these travesties and then continue funding his abuses of the federal government? Why would they allow him to shut down the southern border, knowing that it was not only people from South America immigrating into our country but also radical jihadists from these war-torn areas seeking to infiltrate our way life and wage war on our society? How does it make sense that he would refuse to look the real enemy of the West in the face and call it for what it is? Unless of course, it was a part of a larger U.N. plan, carefully crafted and carried out by the submissive U.S. government to aid and abet the appointment of a one world religion by force, crushing all of those who will stand in its way. In other words, check mark, the U.N. is well on its way to deposing Christianity and enslaving humanity not just financially, but religiously as well under the ever-oppressive Sharia Law.

Ladies and gentlemen, whether you believe in the New World Order or not is completely beside the point. What I want you to take away from this analysis is a simple truth: Trump is not the imperialist here, we are. And when I say "we," I am speaking of course about our representatives in Washington, the proverbial "we," if you will.

Donald Trump is a rejection of the imperialist agendas of past Presidents, a small flicker of light in a darkness looming relentlessly for decades. A breath of fresh air that we as the American people desperately need. We all knew that the challenge he would face in office would be great, that the attacks would be dirty and remorseless, but what we cannot do at this point, is tuck our tails and run away.

Trump can still be the President we voted for, but as long as we the people accept the wild accusations against him as fact, including the idea that he is an imperialist, when Obama modeled the true definition of the word and Trump is a direct repudiation of his ideology, then he will be able to do nothing but constantly defend his honor.

My friends, Obama and Hilary Clinton have returned to the political stage to gear up for the midterm elections and steer the broken Democratic Party back towards a position of power; back toward a system of global interference, U.N. submission, and an agenda for world governance. Let us remember who the real tyrants are in the info war we are now immersed in. Because while we are busy debating whether or not Trump is a fascist and a dictator, the Donald is on the frontline, Trumping Imperialism.

Chapter Five
The Future of Politics

Donald Trump is President. I think the more I say the phrase, the more confident I become in the future of our republic. I have to admit that after years of studying politics and becoming more awake to the real corruption existing in the world around us, the more skeptical and negative I have become concerning my opinion on the outlook for our future.

I went into the election in 2016 fully expecting to once again be disappointed in its outcome, but nevertheless, something told me that the American people would not fall prey to another Clinton scheme. The problem is that even though we have won a great victory against the globalists, the war is far from over.

For the first time in decades, America has truly elected a President, one with his own agenda and believe it or not, his agenda is our agenda. Do you think the establishment will sit idly by while he restores the greatness of the United States? Do you think they will eventually give in and just implement his agenda as they did with Obama? Obama was part of the system, Trump is not. You can be sure that his plight is an uphill battle and he will only succeed with the support of his base.

Trump bravely chanted to the wanting masses, "Americanism, not globalism, will be our credo!" And since taking office, he has been working to uphold that statement tirelessly. My fear, however, is that the public is so overrun with propaganda from the left and is tiring so quickly of the scandals painted across our news outlets from his administration, they may lose sight of the real enemy we face. Russia is not that enemy, the conservative movement in the U.S. is not the enemy, and by that same regard, bigotry and racial division are also not the entity with which we are at war.

Regardless of how hard the liberals fight to incite violence and create unnecessary tension, it is important to remember that these tactics are merely a distraction from the real issues at hand. The country has been sold out to foreign interests, set up on a path to destruction, and being used as the unlimited financial and military resource for the New World Order. With this in mind, we must take the mud-slinging we will no doubt see between now and the midterms with a grain of salt and instead focus on the results from Trump thus far. Contrary to popular belief, they have been substantial, effective, and implemented with only the goal of America first in mind.

Let me ask you this question, would we be better off at this point under an administration led by Hilary Clinton? I think we can agree that a war with Russia would be underway and granted, we may be rubbing shoulders with the heads of Europe, but is that what we really want? Hilary was beholden to the Chinese, to Saudi Arabia, to the New World Order and therefore the question stands, what rights would you have given up at this point in exchange for the first female president? Let me lay out a few items you may be missing had the election gone a different way.

First of all, Hilary Clinton is an enemy of true journalism. There is a reason that CNN has become known as the Clinton News Network and it is not solely due to their biased reporting. The Clintons are known for suppressing the media and operating behind closed doors. Think back to Hilary's campaign, do you remember how many press conferences she gave in secret? How many events did she speak at in which she refused recordings of any kind? I often thought about how nice it would be to hear exactly what she was saying, rather than trying to read between the lines the following day in print journalism. Yet, we had to rely on the unaccredited reporting of main stream news outlets to get any idea of who the real Hilary Clinton was. Can you imagine why it is that the American people felt they could not relate to such an individual?

It was not only Hilary. After all, Obama worked in nearly the exact same manner but yet, the MSM would have you believe that his administration was an open doorway. My friends, the real truth is that Donald Trump is the first truly open President we have seen since, I do not know, Ronald Reagan? Therefore, let us contemplate the existence of the first amendment under Hilary. Do you think we would still have the right to the press after seven months of Clinton? Real journalists might have exposed her back door deals and corrupt favors for pay schemes, why would she not just continue to suppress the media, as she did on the campaign trail? Why not just indict alternative media sources, as she promised to do, by way of strict FCC regulations they would no doubt disregard? Wait, do you not remember when she talked about the dark heart of Alex Jones and how entities like the Drudge Report deserve no place in our society?

I can say to you with the utmost assurance that if Hilary had been elected, your freedom of speech would have been attacked almost immediately. By contrast, Trump has gone to war with the mainstream media, rather than the alternative media. He has promised to disband the fake news syndicate in the U.S. and, though he may enjoy it a little too much, he has not given them a second of relief since taking office. In fact, Trump tweets, to the dismay of most of the Washington establishment, in order to express his freedom to speak openly. Regardless of your feelings on the matter, I think it is extremely important for Trump to use social media to reach the people and I invite him to do so as much as possible.

Now, how about the second amendment? Do you believe that Hilary, the war monger, would have left the right to bear arms intact? With every mass shooting, the liberals, including Hilary, touted the disarming of the American people as if removing a right so long enjoyed and maintained as a staple of our democracy, would repair the damage done by liberal brainwashing in a few short decades. Do you not think that the shootings we have seen, increased recently under the Obama administration, cannot be more logically attributed to the increase in racial division, propagated through the White House, violent media, the poisoning of the food supply affecting brain function, and other environmental factors, rather than simply the issue of responsible gun ownership?

In the early 1800's, domestic issues were solved with a gun duel at high noon, in the middle of the street. How is it that only now, with so much social evolution under our belts, we are suddenly unable to handle self-armament? I choose to believe that it is instead an agenda created by a government wishing to further oppress its citizens, first requiring a mass disarming of the population, peddling the need to take the guns, rather than a citizenry no longer capable of being responsible.

Europe has disarmed it citizens and I think we can see how that has backfired. With every terror attack, one can only contemplate the reduction in casualties, if someone in the crowd has been armed, if only someone had been able to fire back. Ladies and gentlemen, the criminals will always find a way to commit crimes. No one in Europe is allowed to privately own a gun and therefore, the terrorists have been running around stabbing people to death and running large vehicles into crowds of innocents. Shall we now ban the knives? Should we ban cars?

Oh wait, the NWO is already pushing for autonomous vehicles. Did you think that was merely a scientific advancement? Let me ask you this, would you get into a car you had no control over? I do not even like being in a car when I can drive it, I certainly will not subject myself to a death trap controlled by a computer program.

Here is the point, Donald Trump spoke at the NRA because he believes in freedom. He believes in the American way and he understands that a disarmed population is one that will subject itself to rule from a foreign oppressor. You can be sure that the second amendment, and for that matter, the Constitution as a whole, will be preserved under Donald Trump and I submit to you that this is a very different story than we would have seen at this point under Hilary Clinton. We made a good choice, we have taken a step in the right direction, and the tables are starting to turn. We merely need to take a breath, support our President, and work toward making America great again!

With that said, assuming that Trump is allowed to get back to his agenda, I wonder what the future of politics will look like in America, after the influence of such a polarizing administration? Do you think that it will truly change the status quo of Washington? That it will hand the rule of law back to the people, for the people? After all, this is why we elected Trump, this is what we expect from the next eight years. I am only curious to find out what an ideal American society will look like, after so many years of globalist occupation.

What I expect to see is a new confidence of the American public in taking part in office. We saw record numbers of people come out to vote for Trump, but I believe that this is only the first step. My hope is that the future will show a new trend with the people not only having an interest in voting and who their representatives running for office are, but themselves starting campaigns, speaking out, and attempting to embody a role in the real legislative process; a responsibility for governing ourselves. After all, democracy is the act of self-governance, but if we allow an outside force to occupy our republic and steer our agenda in a direction that is specifically un-American, then we are not truly governing ourselves. We are instead, merely submitting to the rule of tyrants, whom our forefathers died to liberate us from in the first place.

In the past, Presidential campaigns tallied a cost which broke a billion dollars under Obama and with Hilary it was over two billion. Amazing, is it not? How can any American believe that they would be capable of running for the highest office when the price tag is so unattainable? Interestingly enough, with Donald Trump, that price has been brought down to below 300 million. Can you imagine such an incredible reversal of precedent? Did you even realize that he had spent so much less than Hilary and nevertheless managed to win by a landslide?

While it may still remain a massive undertaking to pay 300 million dollars to run for office, the trend has been shifted, the office is being returned to the people, and Donald Trump has single-handedly changed the definition of a Presidential campaign. The media would have you believe that he is simply polarizing due to the Russian scandal surrounding his administration, but the truth is far more complex.

Trump represents the people of the United States, more so than any President this century, and with that power hedging his position, he has the potential to change the very fabric of what we have grown to understand as modern politics. Just look at the facts. The Rock is now talking seriously about running for President in 2020. Not that I have any interest in seeing Dwayne Johnson in the White House, but nevertheless, it is an idea that would have been totally foreign only a few years ago.

Nationwide, businessmen and women, statesmen, engineers, journalists, and even IT structure experts the likes of John McAfee are starting to throw in their names and intentions to both run for office and depose the establishment long overdue for a relieve from duty. In addition to that, more and more people are starting to believe that it is possible for them to win the seat, rather than just upsetting the allocation of votes. Can you see the benefit to a Donald Trump in office? Do you believe that the future is bright with such a transformation of common practice? I believe the status quo has indeed been interrupted, shifted in a positive direction, and more than ever I am looking forward to what lies ahead for the American political system. A system free from the cronies, void of negligent budgetary decisions, and one which offers a truly open door policy to the public, concerning legislation and foreign policy.

Following the Trump administration I expect a secure system of borders surrounding our country. I expect a sensible immigration policy which allows those wishing to join our republic entry, but denies those who would prefer to demand assimilation. I expect a private sector governed by a stricter set of anti-trust laws. At this point, I am very curious to see what will happen with the blooming monopoly of Jeff Bezos at Amazon. Hopefully, Trump will step in and put his Justice Department on the case, but it remains to be seen.

Finally, I expect a government which hesitates to sign on to unfair trade agreements and foreign policies dedicated to stealing tax dollars, rather than arranging a deal of mutual benefit. My loyal readers, I hope that you will put as much hope into this administration as I do, because, at the end of the day, a positive attitude toward our current state of affairs will bode much better for the outcome, rather than a constant barrage of attacks and unrealistic expectations. Donald Trump is President, nothing can change that fact at this point. Why not take advantage of this opportunity and use him as the blank slate we the Patriots of America have needed for so long? A slate which can reshape our republic, restore confidence in our markets, and fortify the future of politics with the American people firmly in mind.

www.ingramcontent.com/pod-product-compliance
Lightning Source LLC
Chambersburg PA
CBHW071119280526
45787CB00003B/1093